Fulfilled

Fulfilled

A PERSONAL REVOLUTION IN 7 STEPS

DEIRDRE BOUNDS

PEARSON EDUCATION LIMITED

Edinburgh Gate
Harlow CM20 2JE
Tel: +44 (0)1279 623623
Fax: +44 (0)1279 431059
Website: www.pearsoned.co.uk

First published in Great Britain in 2009

ISBN: 978-0-273-72552-7

British Library Cataloguing-in-Publication Data
A catalogue record for this book is available from the British Library

Library of Congress Cataloging-in-Publication Data

Bounds, Deirdre.
    Fulfilled : a personal revolution in 7 steps / Deirdre Bounds.
        p. cm.
    Includes bibliographical references and index.
    ISBN 978-0-273-72552-7 (pbk.)
    1. Self-help techniques. 2. Change (Psychology) 3. Self-actualization (Psychology)
I. Title.
    BF632.B65 2009
    158.1—dc22

                                                                2009014456

10 9 8 7 6 5 4 3 2 1
13 12 11 10 09

Text design by Julie Martin

Typeset in Ehrhardt MT Std 12/16pt by 3
Printed and bound in Great Britain by Ashford Colour Press Ltd, Gosport, Hants

The publisher's policy is to use paper manufactured from sustainable forests.

THANK YOU

Bryan, the love of my life
Mum, for giving us your life
Friends in 12 Step programmes, you gave me back my life
You, for being willing to change your life

Deirdre Bounds is one of the UK's most prominent female entrepreneurs. After completing her degree at Leeds University, and a short spell drifting from job to job, she left the UK to become an English teacher in Tokyo. It was here that she was introduced to the 12 Step programme. She subsequently travelled and worked in China, Australia and Greece.

Returning to the north of England in 1994, Deirdre became a youth worker and a stand-up comedienne. Realising that there was no future in either profession, she started i-to-i.com – which was to become the world's largest gap year company – from a bedsit in Leeds. Over a period of 11 years she built this into a multinational, award-winning organisation, selling it in 2007 to a FTSE 100 Company.

Deirdre is a much sought-after motivational speaker and winner of many prestigious business awards. She is the Chairperson of three companies, is Patron of Marie Curie Cancer Care in West Yorkshire and is the Ambassador for Enterprise for Young people in Yorkshire and Humber.

Since 1991, she has studied and practised the principles of the programme contained in this book and continues to do so.

www.deirdrebounds.com

CONTENTS

•••

ACKNOWLEDGEMENTS

...

These pages could not have arrived in your hands without the help of many wonderful people, so a huge thank you to:

Bryan, my husband, whose knowledge and fine mind shone through as he helped me to write many of the chapters.

Larry Gaines from The Kelly Foundation in Arkansas, who sat with us in Yorkshire, gave his wisdom freely and drank us out of Yorkshire Tea.

Joyce, my friend and guide, for helping to steer me through the last 17 years.

Rachael Stock from Pearson, who had faith in this book all along and who has done a sterling edit.

My sister Liz and brother Ian, who were forced to read every word and comment at least five times on each chapter.

Bill Wilson for coming up with this Programme.

AA World Services for their support and allowing me to reprint the 12 Steps.

Most of all, I thank the people who have given their time and knowledge to me through the years, especially the guys in the Leeds and Harrogate meetings. I love you all.

Ten per cent of author's earned royalties will go to Deirdre's chosen charities.

ME AND WHY I WROTE THIS BOOK

• • •

Do you ever feel there must be more to life? Or that you might be missing something? Maybe you've achieved quite a lot, but you're always pressured and there doesn't seem to be much real pleasure in your life. Maybe you feel frustrated at a lack of success in your career or in your personal life. Perhaps you've got problems that you can't seem to deal with.

Many of us sometimes feel generally flat, empty, stressed, anxious, or wonder why we're quick to lose our temper or seek refuge in whatever vice we have (and let's face it, there are plenty to choose from). If you've ever thought there must be a better way, then this is the book for you.

As a society, we're not really very happy any more. We have more possessions now than both our parents and grandparents put together, and statistics show that we're more miserable than ever.

Everyone is chasing success and is off doing their own thing. We've bought into the idea that we need to satisfy our emotional needs with what is outside us. This could be material stuff, other people's opinions, the desperation of romantic love, our body image, our career or whatever. And we keep on coming back to try to get more. We've forgotten our connectedness in our chase for more stuff and this imposed isolation is slowly destructive.

We are restless, irritable and discontented. We don't know why, often we don't know who we really are – and most concerning of all is that we probably don't even know it.

In short, we are not fulfilled.

This book is not about success or getting rich, nor is it about selling you a 'quick-fix' solution to everything. Neither will you be brainwashed or offered well-worn NLP techniques to change the way you think.

In this book you will find a solution-oriented, problem-solving process that will give you a code for living a better kind of life, and show you how to handle any and every situation.

This book is about figuring out who you really are, why you feel the way you do, and finding fulfilment within yourself and the world you live in. Once you've grasped the basics of this, then feel free to go and get success books, life coaches, attend 'breakthrough experience' workshops, and neurolinguistic pro-gramme yourself all you like. But only then will they be of any real use to you.

This book is about change. The programme within it will guide you using practical steps to be at ease with yourself, to be the person you were always meant to be, and still can be. Once you know the truth about yourself, and therefore about others, you can then discover your own path to success and achievement.

If you choose to just read this book (as opposed to putting your efforts into working through the full programme) then it will work like many 'change your life'-type books – you will find ideas and inspiration and insight that will help you improve your life. Some points will stick with you and you'll think differently and that'll have a positive effect on you and your relationship with others. However if you choose to actually follow the programme, do the exercises and put yourself fully into the Steps, then you will experience the full power of the book and the level of change will be nothing short of a personal revolution. Not everybody will want to put the full effort in, and that's fine, you'll still gain something and find it useful and positive. If you do give it the full 100 per cent, however, then what you'll get out of it will be a deep, far-reaching, life-enhancing experience that goes way beyond anything you'll find in any other book. The choice is yours!

• WHAT DOES A FULFILLED PERSON • LOOK LIKE?

We come across them occasionally. We like them, we're attracted to them, though the reason why sometimes escapes us. Perhaps you're lucky enough to work with one, or are married to one, or met one on a train, or in the supermarket, or read about one in a magazine; maybe one teaches your children, or maybe one of your children is one.

I'm referring to 'one' as there aren't many around. Being fulfilled takes both knowledge and self-searching. For most of us, that means we have to put some effort in. Some people just seem to be able to go through life serenely knowing who they are, what they want, and they always seem to attain it. 'Lucky', they often get called. They aren't lucky. They understand and accept something. And that something is precisely what this book is about. It's about a way to find the truth about who you are and then what it is you want to 'get' for your life.

Do you think you are one of the 'lucky' ones? Or do you think that fulfilment eludes you in some way? Take a look at these questions and answer as honestly as you can. And I do mean honestly. You can't move forward until you know and accept where you are.

AM I FULFILLED?

Do I feel discontented with my life today?

When things go wrong, does it stress me out?

Do I take pleasure in gossiping about others?

Am I fearful that I won't get what I want out of life?

Do I feel that life is a party, and I'm on the outside looking in?

Do I focus more on my problems than the good things?

Am I my own worst enemy?

Do I feel that life is routine and uninspiring?

Do I wish I had more energy to enjoy my day?

Do I want to change my body size?

Am I concerned about my reputation and what others think of me?

Am I resentful or fearful about anyone or anything today?

If you've answered 'no' to the majority of these questions, return this book and get a refund. If you've answered 'yes' to most of these questions, then good news. You've just begun the journey that will lead to personal fulfilment.

• WHAT DO I KNOW ABOUT ALL THIS • ANYWAY?

In my mid-20s, I was in Japan working as an English teacher. I'd left England, blaming my unhappiness on everybody and everything – other than me. I was fed up and had a gloomy outlook on life, but if you met me you'd think I had it all going for me: fun personality, good-looking, reasonably intelligent and travelling the world. But actually I was a lost soul, confused about life, financially and spiritually broke and drifting. I drank too much, smoked around 40 cigarettes a day and lived in fear that somebody would find out about the 'real' me. I had no idea what a 'fulfilled' person was, and I had less inclination to find out because I was out to get all I could out of life.

Things went from bad to worse, and I found myself in a downward spiral. At rock bottom, I was in all kinds of trouble and probably as far from fulfilled as it's possible to get.

The turning point came when I found a different way to live – one that is infinitely more profitable than the relentless chase for success. But ironically, it's this different way to live that has catapulted me to great success in business and given me considerable wealth. It has also given me the opportunity to meet a wonderful man, my husband Bryan, have two children, Frankie and Ava, be closer to my family, give to society and generally be OK with the world.

I've watched many others who are on this same journey. They find the power to be fulfilled whatever life throws at them, small or large. It sees them through even when battling with serious illness, or after losing their job or a loved one. They overcome enormous setbacks and get through seemingly hopeless situations with grace and serenity.

We'll come on to how they do this soon, but for now let's just take a look at how following the programme in this book will improve your view of yourself and the world. You'll:

- discover what is really holding you back in life and how to 'let it go';
- uncover, discover and discard what is blocking you from being fulfilled with your life;
- improve your relationships by understanding how your actions affect others;
- make amends to those to whom you have done wrong, including yourself;
- find the power within you and learn how to continue this programme for life through simple self-searching techniques;
- feel so good that you'll want to give it away.

This may sound like too big a lump to swallow. I thought so too, but I grasped this new way of living as though my life depended on it... to be fair it probably did, because without it I would probably have been dead within a few years of hitting rock bottom.

• WHO WILL THIS BOOK HELP THE • MOST?

You don't *have* to hit rock bottom for this programme to transform your life, but it helps if you've reached a point where you've had enough of living the way you are living, and not knowing why you feel like you do. There is a saying '*Are you sick and tired of being sick and tired?*' If so, you're at the turning point, and this is a great time for you to read this book.

This programme that you are about to embark on is simple, but not easy. What's required of you to make it work?

Three things only:

1 **Willingness:**
   You've shown this already just by starting to read this book.
2 **Open-mindedness:**
   All I ask of you is to keep an open mind. You may want to reject some of the exercises and information that you read. That's probably your ego talking, but we'll get to that later.
3 **Rigorous honesty:**
   Chances are you aren't being exactly truthful with yourself, though you might not realise it. It does take courage to be honest and to get real.

Nice and simple, just as I promised.

Close your eyes, take a deep breath, know that today is the worst day of your life, because it's all about to change.

So let's go.

• PROOF OF THE PUDDING •

(HOW DO I KNOW THIS STUFF WORKS?)

TOKYO: NOVEMBER 1991

It was only 3 p.m. and I'd already drunk the equivalent of four pints of beer from tiny Japanese bottles. I was 28 years old and had been working in Japan as an English teacher for more than six months. But even though I was surrounded by people, the loneliness and isolation I felt inside was tearing me apart. My fellow teachers bored me, my pupils were dull and I had no boyfriend or any real friends to distract me from myself.

I started to cycle with wobbly concentration to meet a teacher colleague of mine, Randy, at the Onsen, a traditional Japanese bathhouse. I was desperate to have someone to talk to since I had spent the previous night, like many of the nights before it, alone with only several bottles of wine and my thoughts to keep me occupied. He was the only bit of company I was going to have all day and nothing was going to stop me from meeting him.

But while my determination was strong, my balance wasn't playing ball. I turned a corner at the supermarket near where I lived. The front wheel of my bike began to wobble and I fought with the upright handlebars to keep it straight. In slow motion, my bike lurched to the left and I flew off, rolling down into one of the paddy fields that lined the road, followed swiftly by my bike. Before I knew it I was lying on my back in a pool of muddy water.

I was soaked through to my skin, and I gasped before releasing a high-pitched scream of shock and annoyance. I pushed the crumpled bike from on top of me and staggered to my feet. I looked down and saw that the sticky brown mud of the rice fields had coated my white jeans and T-shirt. Stumbling around drunkenly, I was unsure what to do with myself. I turned back to face the road and saw a group of Japanese onlookers. There were seven or eight of them, some wearing perfectly wrapped kimonos, their faces painted with immaculate traditional Japanese make-up. Their mouths gaped wide open, outlined in strong red lipstick as they surveyed me dripping in mud.

I couldn't tell if they were laughing at me or if they were disgusted and shocked by what they saw: a white woman, standing knee deep in a soggy rice field, her hair and clothes matted with mud, in the bright afternoon sunshine.

'F*** off!' I shouted, the rage building up inside me. It was mixing with the alcohol already in my system, making me so dizzy I could barely stand.

'I f****** hate you all! I f****** hate this place. I f****** hate the Japanese.'

The expletives poured out of me. Years of pent-up anger, self-disgust and unhappiness flowed out of my mouth and I was powerless to stop it.

'What the f*** are you looking at?' I screamed, staggering as I bent to pick up clumps of mud to throw at them. But I knew what they could see. They saw my shame and humiliation. I may as well have been standing there naked, I felt so vulnerable.

LONDON: SEPTEMBER 2006

The weather was surprisingly mild. I was in London's financial district, walking towards the 20-storey glass-fronted European headquarters of Ernst & Young, flanked on either side by two corporate financiers – they looked like the *Blues Brothers* in posh suits. As I got to the revolving door, I caught my breath; this was a defining moment in my life. I just couldn't believe that somebody like me, who 14 years previously had been a dejected, broken wretch, could be presenting the travel company that I had founded to a FTSE 100 company who were interested in buying it.

A few months later, it hit me that I had just sold the company for many millions of pounds. I was baffled. Just how had this happened? How did I go from calamity, hopelessness and crippling fear to a place where I could build a worldwide company with no commercial experience, and on top of that have a fulfilled personal life?

How did I make it from rock bottom to a place infinitely better in every conceivable way? That's what this book is about. But this is how it started. . .

About a week after I'd flung mud at the Japanese, I was introduced to the 12 Step programme. Here I found people who had problems like mine, but more importantly, they had similar feelings about themselves and life. As I sat in that room in Tokyo I saw the 12 Step programme on the wall. I didn't really 'get' the Steps, they looked alien. They were strange to me because they were pointing towards a way of life that was exactly the opposite of the way I was living.

But something had to change, and I was ready to try anything. Whatever it was had to be better than the way I was living. With all the energy I could muster, I went to work. . .

At this point you might be thinking: 'What has this got to do with me? I don't have a drink problem.'

Here's why it's got everything to do with you, and everything to offer all of us and here's why I'm writing this book: I've come to realise that the 12 Steps are actually what changed my whole life in every possible way. The 12 Steps have become so ingrained in my life that without doubt it's this very same process that took me from career doldrums to becoming a self-made millionaire, and it's this same process that helped me to create the happiest possible home and family life, and find real fulfilment and success in most areas of my life.

And it's not just true for me – this is a programme for living that millions of people use on a daily basis to deal with everything that life throws at us.

The 12 Step programme is so much more than a way out of obsessive and compulsive behaviours. It's the most powerful 'change your life' programme that exists. The root of it might be as old as the hills, but the incredible thing is that its power is not being felt by all the millions of people it could help, because outside of those with an alcohol problem or other addiction, very few people know anything about it.

The time has come to change all that. This book is designed to reveal how to change your life in ways you never thought possible, by sharing a distilled version of the most powerful change programme in existence today.

ABOUT THE PROGRAMME

• • •

'On the 10th June 1935, when two alcoholics met and stayed sober, there evolved the 12 Step program by which these recovered alcoholics were to live... *If mankind lived by the same 12 Step program, mankind's inhumanity to mankind would not exist.'*

Henry Kissinger's view of the most important event of the twentieth century

This programme for living has been inspired by the 12 Steps of Alcoholics Anonymous (AA) that has changed lives across the world. For simplicity, it has been distilled into a straightforward 7 Step programme. Remember, this programme can help anybody, regardless of who and where you are, or what particular issues or problems you face.

• WHAT THIS PROGRAMME CAN DO • FOR YOU

If you're honest, open-minded and willing to do the work that's ahead (and it's not easy), this programme will give you a life beyond your wildest dreams. Many people who have followed it say that until they started practising these principles they were merely existing instead of living.

You will uncover who you really are and be able to truly look at yourself, be more accepting and less afraid or angry. *Life will be more fulfilling, not something to be endured or mastered, just to be lived.* This simple set of life principles will bring you untold happiness.

We're not talking Pollyanna stuff here, we're talking about a courageous way of living that will help you to:

- feel happier
- accept yourself and others
- remove age–old resentments
- lift low self-esteem
- connect better to society and the people around you
- not regret the past or fear the future
- be more forgiving
- banish unnecessary fear
- get out of debt
- communicate more effectively
- work out who you are and what you want
- gain true fulfilment in all areas of your life
- reclaim your humanity.

And OK, I did say this was all about 'being' and not 'getting', but frankly if you get cracking on this programme, and learn how to understand yourself and reconnect with the world around you, anything is possible.

• WHY HAS THIS ALL BEEN KEPT • SO QUIET?

The true appreciation of the power of the 12 Step programme and how it works is understandably lacking, as most people who follow it, and whose lives are transformed by it, remain anonymous.

These 12 Step followers are not anonymous out of shame, but part of the philosophy they are now living suggests that it's much better for the human ego to be more humble, rather than shouting about themselves.

The programme works through attraction rather than promotion. Alcoholics Anonymous and all other 12 Step programmes don't advertise, they wait for people to find them. So the 12 Step programme works by quietly being available to those who are willing to change their lives. The downside is that outside of those with particular problems, few would actually find it, as the groups are geared around a particular problem/ situation.

That's where this book comes in. It's specifically adapted to work for you – whatever your life is like.

POWER TO THE PEOPLE

'So what's that got to do with me?' I hear you say. 'I'm not an alcoholic.'

What I'm talking about here is *power*. If these steps can help the most selfish, self-centred, and by their own admission 'self-destructive' people and assist them in finding a useful and whole way of life, you too can use these powerful steps to improve your life. You don't need to consider yourself 'broken', 'lost' or 'hopeless', these steps are so powerful in their application that if followed they can help you gain a level of confidence and serenity that you probably can't ever remember experiencing – ever.

So why do we need more power? We're talking about a different kind of power than we normally think about. We've all been living by 'self-propulsion', as AA founder Bill Wilson put it, with each person 'like an actor who wants to run the whole show' (*Alcoholics Anonymous*, p. 60). Sometimes it works, but in many cases it puts us in conflict with others.

In his remarkable book *Power vs Force* the renowned physician and researcher David Hawkins put it this way: '85% of humanity live by force'. That means the majority of the population are guided by what psychiatrists call the 'emergency' emotions: shame, guilt, fear, pride, desire, anger and resentment. Clearly, 85 per cent is a big percentage, which means you and I are not alone in how we see, feel and react to the world. Look around you, wherever you are, in the office, on the train, in the doctor's waiting room, in the park – of every ten people you see, at least eight struggle with being human. Outwardly they may exude confidence, but our ego is very adept at putting up a protective front so that the world doesn't see us as we think we are. Be gentle with them as well as yourself, they don't understand what's going on as much as you might not.

• SO HOW DOES IT WORK? •

When he was asked how the 12 Step programme worked, Bill Wilson replied: 'It works very well.' He knew that, as a programme of action, the only way to fully appreciate its effectiveness is to have gone through it, and realise its impact.

Basically, the Steps allow us to admit that we're human, discover aspects of ourselves over which we have no control, and grow beyond those limitations by asking for help (being humble enough to ask for help is absolutely crucial – no one can go through a big change in isolation).

So we're talking about a degree of open-mindedness, and a lot of courage and willingness.

Besides these, here are the tools you'll need:

- the guts to admit that you're not in control;
- maturity to take responsibility for your feelings and actions;
- honesty in admitting to yourself your mistakes and personality flaws;
- the integrity to admit that you're wrong;
- the sensibility to realise that there are no quick fixes and that you're working this one day at a time;
- the yearning for getting more balance in your life.

• AS OLD AS MANKIND •

The 12 Steps are principles for living, nothing more and nothing less. The principles themselves are as old as mankind. They have never changed. They are as reliable as the laws that govern science, and once we understand and practise these principles we can live better lives and accomplish great things.

I'm not pumping out a new philosophy or success theory. I agree with Joe McQuany, who founded one of the largest treatment centres in the US. In his marvellous book, *The Steps We Took*, he says that few people seem able or keen to teach us the basic principles of life. 'The Twelve Steps don't have "don'ts" they have "do's". That's what principles are; guidelines for what to do.' The reward for doing them, he goes on to say, 'is simple: it's harmony, it's happiness. . . it's contentment.'

• FROM 12 TO 7 STEPS •

So, why are we just looking at 7 Steps when it's a 12 Step programme, I hear you asking. Good question. Actually, all 12 Steps are covered by the 7 Steps outlined in this book. As an introduction to this powerful new way of living, I hope that breaking it down into seven digestible chunks will be a simpler and more practical way to absorb this information.

• YOU'RE NOT ALONE •

Since it's like the first day at school and most of you will be starting afresh, there is also an interactive website, www.thepersonalrevolution.net, which is a valuable tool for sharing with like-minded people and finding a guide or coach as you work through the Steps.

If you find yourself less than buoyant at the thought of a guide or coach, and think you'd rather keep this to yourself, if we don't mind, then just hold on a minute. Let's be brutally frank: if you could become fulfilled by yourself, you probably wouldn't be reading this book. But none of us are Buddhas here, we all need help. And although you may not realise it yet, you're going to be helping many other people. And the rewards for that are immeasurable. So if you can possibly stay open to the idea, try at this point to consider asking for and accepting help along the way. Yes, I know it doesn't come naturally to everybody, and is really quite uncomfortable for some, but it really does make a difference, and it's a significant part of the shift towards a more fulfilled life.

If you choose to ask for some assistance, then I suggest you look to either a trusted friend, mentor, coach, community leader, member of the clergy, counsellor or other person – whoever you feel most comfortable with. You may be able to find a virtual one on www.thepersonalrevolution.net. This person will share your journey and offer impartial advice and assistance. Think about who you would really trust to share this information with. Don't worry if you can't really think of a person for now, you'll find one. In AA, new members often seek out people with longer sobriety to help take them through the programme, so finding a virtual guide is not as weird as you may think.

If the thought of doing the suggested exercises and finding a guide are currently just too bizarre or too much like hard work, then think of it this way: if you want to learn to drive, you find an instructor who'll show you the ropes. And if you want a change in your life, you go to the gym and pump weights or go to night school for years to improve yourself. This programme is like that, and it doesn't really matter if you like it or not – or are even antagonistic to the idea, it's the result that you're after.

Finally, do you know what I'd really hope to do? I'd like to take you from the position you are in right now in life and expand the possibility of what your life can be for you. I want to try to offer you a way that will give you genuine freedom that is lasting. To be free from what limits you in life, you have to be free from what you think limits you. *Why settle for less when working these steps can offer you more?*

Step One

WHAT'S THE PROBLEM?

• • •

If all you ever do is all you've ever done, then all you'll ever get is all you ever got.

Old Texan saying

Step 1 is about admitting that you're unfulfilled, that you probably don't know why, and that you'll never be able to become fulfilled the way you are going and by doing the things that you've always done.

What's keeping you from being fulfilled is you. You're the problem. And trying to fix yourself – with lists of goals, affirmations, positive thinking and wishes – doesn't work because you don't really know what's wrong. Step 1 tells you to stop and name the problem, find the truth and admit defeat. It sounds negative, but it's actually the first step to reclaiming your power.

• • •

• ACCEPTANCE •

Marcus Aurelius, the ancient Roman emperor and philosopher, probably had more crap days than I can imagine. I like the way he put it:

> And why is it so hard when things go against you? If it's imposed by nature, accept it, and stop fighting it. And if not, work out what your own nature requires, and aim at that, even if it brings you no glory.

We're largely on a collision course with ourselves and with the world. And we don't like or understand it when things don't go our way. Peppered with the occasional highs, life is shot through with fears, anger, envy, frustrations, anxieties, and the feeling of being out of control.

Or as the American philosopher Henry David Thoreau said: '*The mass of men lead lives of quiet desperation.*'

And people... wouldn't the world be great if everybody would just let you do what you want to do and be what you want to be? Instead they all want things out of this world as well – and often that interferes with your life as their needs get in the way of yours. That wise Roman Marcus Aurelius comes back again: 'And why should we feel anger at the world? As if the world would notice.'

This is the problem: we're all scrapping for our share of love, power, prestige and material stuff as if our lives depended on it.

• A LITTLE BIT OF TRUTH •

What you're searching for here is the truth, the truth about yourself: why you do the things you do and why you feel the way you feel. Here's one bit of truth that I've learned: I'm powerless over many, if not most, things in my life. I can't fix them, I can't do them and I can't see them. I am powerless over them. It's the same with us all. The trouble is, there's a voice inside your head that tells you that you can't accept this. So you just keep on doing the same things and hoping that your wrong solutions will somehow make it all right, but that's pretty unlikely, given that you don't even know what the underlying problem really is.

Let me give you an example. At one point in my life I was powerless over my fear of being alone. I had just met my husband Bryan in New York and instantly fell in love with him. He was everything I had ever wanted and dreamed of in a guy. He was kind, gentle, intelligent, funny and, to cap it all off, good-looking. The problem was, I lived in England and he lived in New York. I had met the man I wanted to marry. We had a long-distance, transatlantic romance, fuelled by calls and emails. He came to England and we had a great week visiting the castles of Northumberland and then I visited him in New York.

Finally the relationship became so difficult that Bryan gave me that old chestnut of, 'Let's just be friends.' I was heartbroken. Almost every minute of every day I would wait in hope for a message and was desperate to contact him, but I didn't want to frighten him off. My whole day was consumed with Bryan in my mind; I couldn't stop talking about him, and when people began to stop listening it made me feel even more alone. Nothing interested me. I felt terribly lonely and I just couldn't believe that my hope of finding my soulmate was gone – and actually terrified me. There was no point, and I was going to be alone all of my life.

So what was my problem? Was it the fact that I was heart-broken? No, my problem was that I was powerless over the insane behaviour that the situation had triggered in me. It made me afraid of being alone, I felt I had to control the situation, and I could not let it go during any waking moment – and the reason for this (although I couldn't see it at the time) was because it touched on one of my deepest issues, my fear of abandonment.

You may be thinking that you're not like that, and that you would never get in such a state over a man/woman. And of course that's true, you might not. But if you're feeling a strong level of disquiet or lack of fulfilment in your life then you'll probably have other situations, maybe work-based, maybe in your home life, where your behaviour in certain situations is far from ideal, and the chances are that you don't know what your particular issue really is. You might see some of the symptoms of your problem, for example unrealistic ambitions, overeating, overspending, controlling people, but in all probability, unless you are incredibly self-aware, you aren't clear on what's at the root of it.

But that's OK. If you *know* you don't know exactly what's wrong, but are willing to take responsibility and accept that you're the problem, then you don't need to know any more to start putting it right. In other words, you're never really a victim of the world around you. As absurd as it may be to believe, you are always responsible for how you see and react to things. It's simple:

You need to give up on the problem and realise your powerlessness.

Only by admitting your powerlessness will you actually find power. It's about giving up to gain – yes, I know that sounds odd, but bear with me and all will become clear.

Here's another example. As a young woman I used to smoke 40 cigarettes a day (that's right, 40!). I tried to give up many times but couldn't kick the habit. Each time I'd quit, I would last perhaps a couple of days, more often a couple of hours. When I'd light up again, I'd always beat myself up that I didn't have the willpower. The truth was I was trying to force myself into quitting, when I needed to just surrender to the power that cigarettes had over me. It was only when at 27 I began to get pains in my chest, my clothes stank, my apartment walls were yellow and my fingers were turning an interesting shade of mustard that I accepted that smoking was ruining my health and making my life unmanageable. I surrendered to the power of cigarettes then. I admitted that they were more powerful than me and 'gave in' and 'gave up'. I haven't had a cigarette since.

But let's not think that powerlessness is about addictive and obsessive behaviour. It's about life. Recently I was having lunch with a friend. She works in the very competitive world of recruitment and said business was tough. I listened to her as patiently as I could while she complained about lack of customers, her manager (who hadn't delivered on his promises) and her work colleagues (who were all lazy and only talked about their relationships, their forthcoming weddings or who was due to make the next cup of tea). After close to an hour of this negativity I suggested that perhaps she needed to take responsibility for how she viewed these people and events, including her need to control everything. Eventually she agreed with me and finally said, 'You know, I've just got to accept that I'm powerless over the economy – I can't force people to recruit, I'm powerless over my boss – I can't make him give me what he promised, and I'm powerless over my work colleagues – I can't control what they talk about or do.' She went on to accept that she was the control freak who had a PhD in criticising others and she needed to lighten up and let them go. Thankfully, once we hit the after-lunch coffee a chink of a smile came through.

This Step works in any area of your life, and with any problem.

Personally, I can be powerless over authority figures, my temper, my jealousy and financial insecurity. And when I'm right in the middle of these problems, I can't see the *truth*. And it's only when I uncover and accept the *truth* about my problem that I can look for a solution.

The really frustrating thing is that we're our own saboteurs – it's not that success and fulfilment escape us, we're given plenty of opportunity, but somehow we either ignore it or destroy it. How many of us go from job to job, relationship to relationship, town to town only to arrive in the new location exactly the same person as we left the last one? It's unrealistic and unreasonable to expect our life to change if we refuse to see our part in the problem and accept responsibility for ourselves. I did the same when I left the UK for Japan. I arrived at Tokyo airport exactly the same person as I left England and the thrill of the big city soon wore off as my old behaviours and low-grade angst kicked in.

It's like we keep on trying to get through the same locked door: we've tried climbing over, sliding under and picking the lock. We've even taken to banging our head on it over and over with the same result. Why not go next door? It's open.

• WHAT IS 'DOING YOUR HEAD • IN' TODAY?

Is it your:

- money
- family
- job
- colleagues
- superior/subordinate
- partner
- neighbours
- loneliness
- friends

- health
- body image
- depression
- self-confidence
- goal failures
- career
- life in general.

• DO YOU HAVE OVERDEPENDENCE • ON ANY OF THE FOLLOWING?

- work (either overwork, no work or procrastination)
- people (being controlled or controlling)
- food (too much/too little)
- money (miser or spendthrift)
- cigarettes
- alcohol/drugs
- your reputation or outward appearance
- sex
- material things
- success (whatever that means to you).

The list of human issues is endless – I've only mentioned the obvious ones. The key is to know that you are powerless over many things in life. Then you can fix the issue.

But this sounds so simple, isn't it obvious? Sadly, no, not to most of us. The one thing that stops you from moving forward is your 'ego'. We'll fully get to know your ego in Step 2, but for now your ego is simply an idea of who you are that you carry around with you. It feeds you the juice which tells you that you have the answers, you're in control of your life and can control the lives of others, and you don't need help.

If you choose to take this first Step then you'll experience one of life's great paradoxes: that through getting out of the control room of life and accepting your powerlessness, you'll be open to receiving great strength and power. Conversely, if you don't take this liberating step there's a good chance that you'll probably continue to wallow around just hoping things will work out, that your luck will change and perhaps other people will change your life *for you*. If you do take this step, however, then a sense of the possible happens – because you're not grappling to control events. I realise that giving up control can feel uncomfortable and alien, weak even, but let me promise you, it is not weak, it is the first strength.

• FEELINGS •

What we've been talking about here are feelings and attitudes: pride, anger, fear, self-pity, guilt, resentment, low self-esteem. They drain you, they block you, and you might say that your whole problem has to do with being powerless over your feelings.

What this book will do is give you ways to become aware of these feelings and liberate yourself from them. The result of this unblocking of your mind is that you will raise your consciousness to a level where you can start to be more fulfilled.

That's the whole point of this book: to raise your level of consciousness, so let's take a close look at consciousness itself.

This next bit is going to blow your mind, and it will be worth the brain ache for the next ten minutes. It's very difficult for me to put into words, but this is one path to understanding why some of us are miserable and some are serene.

THE SCIENCE OF KINESIOLOGY

Have you ever had a long chat with someone and, when they left, you felt lifted and energised? Equally have you been in a room with someone and they left you absolutely drained, weakened and in need of a packet of biscuits?

What you're experiencing first-hand is the power of different levels of consciousness. The scientific method for measuring this is kinesiology. Kinesiology is a well-established science of human movement based on muscle response. This sort of scientific testing has found support throughout the world since the 1970s. The test is simple: a test subject listens to a true statement and has a positive (strong) muscle reaction, and a weak reaction when given a false statement. This test is given by having a person hold out his arm as he listens to a statement, then the researcher tries to push his arm down, measuring the strength of the muscle response. Let's look now at how someone has taken this science one step further and much, much deeper.

David R. Hawkins, MD, PhD, a renowned physician, researcher and advocate of kinesiology, has used this testing with groups of several hundred people at a time with consistent and replicable results. It's as if there was some collective sense of truth that everyone was responding to. It follows therefore that this ability to access a 'database' of all human thought must be innate in all of us.

A COLLECTIVE UNCONSCIOUS

What Dr Hawkins has found is an objective technique for revealing what Carl Jung called the 'collective unconscious' – which means that together, all of us resonate with universal feelings, values and motivations. An easy analogy is the archetypal 'hero' story: a young person starts from a state of naivety, is compelled to go on a journey (usually with the help of a wise person) and arrives at his goal after overcoming hardships and uncertainty. That's why we all loved *Star Wars*, *The Lord of the Rings*, even *Cinderella*. We all cheered Rocky on because his story touched our collective unconscious desire to experience triumph over adversity.

From these universal values and feelings Dr Hawkins has constructed a logarithmically calculated scale of human consciousness, according to how strong and positive an effect they have on us. Simply put, this is a sliding scale, numbered from 20 to 1000, of the most common emotions and attitudes that people have.

At the lowest end of the scale are the emotions of shame and guilt (remember our friend who left us feeling drained?). We gradually move up to the 'emergency emotions' of fear, desire, anger and pride. At this level, we are trying to force our will upon ourselves and others, often with frustrating and destructive results. Dr Hawkins describes this energy as force. It's an energy that does not promote life and it leaves us exhausted because it is constantly seeking more energy to sustain itself (i.e. when we try to force our will upon people or things).

Further up the scale, we come to the emotions of integrity (i.e. courage, willingness, acceptance), where positive changes begin to happen in our life. *Instead of using force, we begin using a constructive energy called power.* If you've managed to get this far in the book, this is what you're aiming for.

Again, climbing upwards on the scale, we come to love, joy and peace – these are the feelings that we all aspire to, and when we meet people who express these in their behaviour we are attracted to them. Now you know why. It's a level where the great characters of history lived and exerted tremendous power: Mahatma Gandhi and Winston Churchill to name a couple. At the top of the scale is what we refer to as 'avatars' (Jesus Christ, Buddha and Krishna spring to mind for those of a religious persuasion).

So in broad terms

Calibrated level	Key motivation	Who benefits?
Below 200	Personal survival and ego	Looking after number 1
200–500	Courage and integrity	Thinking of others
500–700	Love	Happiness of others
700–1000	Joy	Salvation of humanity

Unsurprisingly, the results of this scale also coincide with hierarchical levels of traditional philosophy, psychology and spirituality. More details about this scale can be found in Dr Hawkins's extraordinary book, *Power vs Force.*

According to Dr Hawkins, only 15 per cent of the world's population seem to live on a level above 200.

This book makes a big promise – perhaps the biggest promise that has ever been made to you: in these pages you'll find a code for living that will help you reach personal fulfilment.
The most effective way to achieve fulfilment is to begin working a programme that brings you up to the level of 200 or more: the level of courage and integrity.

Now I'm no scientist or therapist, but I do know that this works, because since 1991 I have chosen to follow a programme for living that gives me the tools to operate at the level of 200 or above. If I'm perfectly honest with you, it didn't happen overnight and it wasn't easy, and to be fair I slip down the scale to below 200 often, but at least now I have the knowledge and I know *how* to get there!

I meet many successful and fulfilled people in my daily business and personal life and the most common attributes I see amongst them all is courage and integrity. The mega-successful people that I occasionally come across have the added attribute of humility. If I ask them the secret of their success they often can't tell me and put it down to their team, their wife or husband, but rarely take credit for it themselves.

There is a theme here, isn't there? Contented people know that life is not about them, and have got their ego out of the way.

Do you know where you are on this scale? If you feel that you may currently be on a level below 200, then remember, 85 per cent of the world's population operate below the level of 200, so you are not alone. And what's more, you now have the chance to change where you are and see what it feels like to live on a different level.

• ENOUGH OF THIS THEORY. . . LET'S • GET STARTED

There's a saying: *You're only as sick as your secrets*. The easiest way to get the ball of change rolling faster for you is to set down on paper the things in your life now and things from the past that are causing you distress, making your life unmanageable, getting in your way and generally contributing to your feeling unfulfilled. This may be a tough task, but remember I said you're not alone? If you feel comfortable you can share any of these exercises with your guide or with like-minded people online at www.thepersonalrevolution.net. It's equally fine if you just want to jot them down in private and never let them see the light of day again. But just write them down. Be honest, courageous and open-minded. Be you.

POWERLESSNESS INVENTORY

What are you powerless to stop doing or thinking? Write down as many examples as you can to show where you have been unable to stop certain behaviours or thoughts. The word powerless is used deliberately here, to help you to list the behaviours that you are unable to stop, even when the consequences are unacceptable. Write the numbers 1 to 10 on a bit of paper, and starting from either now or from your earliest memories, think of at least ten examples, five of which should be as recent as possible. If you end up with more than 10, that's fine. Do actually write these down, rather than just thinking about them. The writing is important as it triggers a release.

For example:

- I'm deeply in debt but I'm afraid to open the bills as they come through the letterbox.
- I gave myself 12 months to get the courage to leave my job and pursue my dream; now it's several years later and I'm still here, and I hate it.
- I know I'm overweight, but I enjoy food and can't stop overeating.
- I always seem to be late for appointments or meetings and it's getting embarrassing.
- My partner criticises me because I'm always on my BlackBerry, even in bed.
- I can't stop using an online dating site, and I'm constantly checking who's interested in me.
- I hate my neighbour so much after she wrote a complaint letter to me that I've recently thrown snails over the fence onto her property.
- I keep sleeping with people from the office and I feel so ashamed and guilty that it's affecting my work.
- I'm so envious of my best friend's seemingly perfect life that I don't want to call her.

Now answer this question honestly:

Do I still believe that someday I'll become fulfilled if I keep doing it my way?

Answer: YES, Keep doing what you're doing (and refer to page 1)
Answer: NO, you may be at the point where you see that you are powerless and ready to give in.

If you've admitted your powerlessness and the consequences, then it's fair to say that you've exhausted your personal power to fix this. The solution therefore must come from a power beyond yourself.

STEP IN BRIEF

- Using force to solve a problem doesn't work.
- The first action in overcoming a core problem is to admit that you are powerless over it.
- This opens the door to a new type of power.

S t e p   T w o

THE SOLUTION

• • •

No problem can be solved from the same level of consciousness that created it.

Einstein

If I accept that I have a living problem that I cannot solve myself, then what's the solution? That's what we'll look at in this chapter. First let's look at the core root of our problems (because they are the same for everybody's problems, surprisingly – you'll see), then we'll look at and understand the driver of our problems.

Then the solution will become clear.

● ● ●

• PART 1: THE ROOT AND DRIVER OF • THE PROBLEM

Both you and I, and everybody else you know, are ruled by basic human instincts. These instincts have been with us since the human race began. So to really understand our problem and get a solution we have to understand three things:

1 what the instincts are
2 how we've misused them
3 what is driving us to protect ourselves from seeing the truth about them.

• WHAT ARE THE INSTINCTS? •

What do you think are the basic instincts of human beings? It's an interesting question. Why not put this book down for a moment and see what you come up with? You may intuitively know, but you have possibly forgotten about many instincts, because generally you don't think about them. *You're just like the rest of us operating on autopilot, and have become a 'human doing' rather than a 'human being'.*

According to the dictionary definition (bear with me, this is important), instincts are: an inborn pattern of behaviour characteristic of a species and shaped by biological necessities such as survival and reproduction. Put another way, it means that instincts are biological fixtures just like organs in our body and we need them to survive. Just as we need a heart and lungs for our physical survival, there is no way we can live without these psychological and spiritual survival tools. So, let's take a look at the three basic human instincts:

social instinct

security instinct

sex instinct.

OUR SOCIAL INSTINCT

It's pretty simple for most of us, we want to connect to other people and have a feeling of belonging. This is how humans are wired. And it's probably a good thing for us all – let's face it: with around 6.7 billion people currently living on this planet, you'd be hard pressed to find a solitary spot for any length of time, so the ability to get along with others and get pleasure from being with others is pretty useful. The social instinct shows itself in the following ways:

COMPANIONSHIP: What do we personally need to 'feel' to be OK? Well, even the most ardent individualists want to fit in and be accepted. Whether in a conventional or unconventional way, live or online, we all want to have friends, acquaintances and a family unit (even as a last resort). Nobody likes to feel totally isolated, not for a long period of time anyway. My young nephew summed this instinct up when he told me with great pride that he had 480 'friends' on Facebook!

PRIDE: Well, my young nephew certainly had plenty of this basic instinct with his Facebook news. Pride in ourselves, our work, our family, our house, our country is encouraged. We need this instinct otherwise we wouldn't care to get out of bed and brush our teeth in the morning. In proper proportions, pride can be positive.

PERSONAL RELATIONSHIPS: This is about our friends, relations, work colleagues and people we come across in life (you know, even the people who bump their supermarket trolley into yours, or the assistant in the shop). It's about how we interact, how we form and respond to relationships, from the people we meet every day to those we meet for a fleeting second. Our interaction on a moment-by-moment basis matters to you, to them and to society.

SELF-ESTEEM: Our opinion of ourselves is directly linked to our self-esteem, either high or low. It encompasses beliefs, such as 'I am intelligent' or 'I am stupid', and emotions, such as pride or shame. Our self-esteem can often be seen via our behaviour, so we may exude confidence or caution depending on what we believe about ourselves. This is a very personal belief or emotion.

PRESTIGE: This is how we want society to think about us. Our reputation or importance. Whilst self-esteem is our own opinion of ourselves, prestige is our view of the opinion of others about us.

AMBITION: Ambition is natural and normal. It is our inner drive to gain a reputation and be accepted in society.

OUR SECURITY INSTINCT

At its most basic, this instinct helps us to perform daily tasks to gain the basic necessities to live. If it weren't for our basic needs for security, we wouldn't have a roof over our heads or food in our stomachs. As a species we wouldn't last very long! We also need to feel secure in our emotions. Our security instinct centres around three main areas:

MATERIAL: Ensuring that we have basic shelter and food. We all accept that this instinct is necessary for us to function on a daily basis. In my work, I've travelled to some of the poorest areas on this earth, and the ingenuity of some people astonishes me with their ability to create shelter out of bits of old cardboard and tin. We all do what we can and what we need to do to feel secure.

EMOTIONAL: This is really simple. As human beings we want to be loved or to love. This is the instinct at its most basic. The feelings of emotional safety and security are very much a part of it.

AMBITIONS: Once again, having ambitions and goals is natural. Every human being wants to gain at least enough materially to feel secure for the future.

OUR SEX INSTINCT

You don't need me to tell you about this basic and natural biological impulse. Or do you? This instinct brings about reproduction and keeps us 6.7 billion people busy multiplying – now there's an image for you! I'll keep the three areas we look at here pretty brief.

ACCEPTABLE: This is a basic impulse necessary to humankind. It's normal and necessary for reproduction.

HIDDEN: It feels so good that we long for it, we are motivated to look for it and sometimes this yearning drives us to act in a way that is contrary to society's or our own principles.

AMBITIONS: Our plans and desires are either acceptable or hidden. For most women, there's a biological ambition to find the right man and raise a family. For men, it's probably biologically more driven by a desire to sow their wild oats as widely as possible before settling down and investing in a family.

• AND HERE'S WHERE IT ALL GOES • WRONG. . .

The founder of AA, Bill Wilson, realised that, while 'the basic instincts of life' are necessary to create food, shelter, society and reproduction, these basic instincts not only motivate us, they can begin to dominate us if we *overuse* them or *misuse* them – as most of us do:

> These instincts, so necessary for our existence, often far exceed their proper functions. Powerfully, blindly, many times subtly, they drive us, dominate us, and insist on ruling our lives. Our desires for sex, for material and emotional security, and for an all-important place in society often tyrannize us. When thus out of joint, man's natural desires cause him great trouble. Practically all the trouble there is.

Now here's the really important bit:

> nearly every serious emotional problem can be seen as a case of misdirected instincts. When that happens, our

great natural assets, the instincts, have turned into
physical and mental liabilities.

Bill Wilson, *The Twelve Steps and the Twelve Traditions*, p. 42

• WHAT DO THESE LIABILITIES • LOOK LIKE?

If we listed all these, we could write a new Instinct-Wikipedia. But see if you can find yourself in any of these scenarios:

1 SOCIAL INSTINCTS

COMPANIONSHIP: When I was at university, I remember sitting in the coffee area alone when dozens of students were skipping by me in cliques and groups, and I just felt alone, different and unliked. I was filled with self-pity.

PRIDE: The problem as we all know is that 'Pride goeth before a fall'. Some of us find it hard to ask for help when we really need it, because we're afraid that we won't be seen in as good a light as we think we should. Think about the last time that happened to you or someone you know.

RELATIONSHIP: The next time you stick one finger up to a driver who has cut in front of you, know that it is your basic social instinct that has been affected and momentarily 'infected'.

SELF-ESTEEM: Have you ever said anything stupid or inappropriate and felt embarrassed afterwards, cringing and saying to yourself, 'I can't believe I said that'? We've all felt this blow to our self-esteem.

PRESTIGE: Many people are consumed with what others think of them rather than with what they think of themselves. This is even more pronounced these days with our love of celebrity and all of the clamour for prestige which that brings. Climbing up the corporate ladder, getting that all-important promotion, or wanting to be the head knitter at the knitting circle – we all want others to think well of us and think 'My, hasn't he done well.'

AMBITION: Ambition can be as dangerous a route to good living as it is a safe one, especially if our ambitions put us on a collision course with others on the same road.

2 SECURITY

MATERIAL: We're a funny lot – we humans. Fulfilling our basic needs with shelter and food often isn't enough. We need that blanket of additional security via a bigger house (so we can put more possessions in it), a better car, an expensive designer handbag and more prestige. It's as if we have a hole in our soul which we're trying to fill with stuff outside of us.

EMOTIONAL: This instinct can drive us into two areas: domination or dependence. If we feel insecure, we might wield power and dominate somebody so that we can feel better about ourselves. Or we can place our security in the hands of someone else, by comparing ourselves to them. Whether it's a relationship in the bedroom, the boardroom or the classroom, we've all felt or seen people who were puffed up with power, needy for approval or scared out of their wits.

AMBITIONS: It is when they drive us in the never-ending pursuit of material goods, cars, houses and controlling or needy relationships that they can cause difficulty. . . and all in the quest of 'feeling' secure.

Let's not forget that this need to feel secure is a basic human instinct, it is natural and normal. In other words, we're not all 'weirdos' on the hunt for something we're not supposed to feel, we're just all hunting weirdly for more than we're supposed to get.

3 SEX INSTINCT

It's no coincidence that Sharon Stone's most memorable film is called *Basic Instinct*. The sex instinct is humankind's most powerful drive. In our search to satisfy our deepest needs, we use sex to forge intimate relationships.

But when sex is misused, when we use it selfishly and inconsiderately, this basic instinct can be the most damaging, both to others and ourselves. If we are filled with ambition, we might use sex to prove our strength (or weakness) or attractiveness. When we feel hurt or resentful, we can use sex to get revenge. If our self-esteem is not healthy, we might use sex to punish ourselves, perhaps without realising it.

In the throes of this passion, our mind is a master at helping us to deny and rationalise this destructive behaviour.

> **Every time a person imposes his instincts unreasonably upon others, unhappiness follows.**
>
> Bill Wilson

So there's your lesson in being human, but you probably knew a lot of this already. So what am I telling you this for? It's because once you understand what your basic human instincts are and why you have them, then you'll be able to recognise what happens to all of us poor humans when these basic human needs get threatened or warped. If your instincts are out of sync with what is natural and normal (i.e. if you're getting carried away, wanting more than you should or misapplying the instinct), without fail this will manifest itself in these three areas:

You will form resentments.

You will become fearful.

You will cause harm to others or yourself.

Resentment	Fear	Harms or hurts
Feelings of bitterness, anger and indignation arising from what others have done to you.	Feelings of worry, anxiety, agitation about the past, present or future.	Actions that have resulted in hurt feelings and pain, including financial loss, for other people and yourself.

I'll discuss these more in the next chapter, but it will help you to get familiar with these brief descriptions. These feelings are a big part of what's blocking you from being fulfilled. What I want to do moving forward is to help you to dismantle them and nip these feelings in the bud before they continue to screw up your life. In other words, we want to uncover, discover and discard them.

All of our problems emanate from us trying to satisfy our basic instincts that have gone out of control because these instincts are threatened in some way or another. No one wants to be seen as being insecure, resentful or fearful, so our 'ego' takes over, and comes to the rescue like a knight in shining armour to protect us from actually looking at our part and taking responsibility.

Just as our biological organs can malfunction – which leads us to seek medical help – so too can our basic instincts. When that happens, to whom can we turn to fix them? You can have a go yourself, but it would be like trying to perform open heart surgery on yourself, you just wouldn't do it, would you? (Even if you were the best heart surgeon in the country!) That's the measure of the insanity of trying to fix ourselves. We are forever trying to fix ourselves with ourselves and we just can't do it.

Insanity: doing the same thing over and over again and expecting different results.

Einstein

• AND NOW MEET THE DRIVER OF • OUR INSECURITIES, SIR EGO!

If you've completed your powerlessness inventory at the end of Step 1, you've taken the first step. Now we need to take a look at what is driving our Insecurities and making our lives insane. Insanity comes from the Latin word *sanus*, which means 'healthy'. So while you may smart at being called insane, it's not that bad really. It just means that your mind and therefore your life are unhealthy.

As you'll see, your ego both rules your life and your connection to the world and people around you. We all like to feel connected, but it's when our ego blocks us from the world around us that we create problems and act insanely, well unhealthily at least.

• WHAT IS THE EGO? •

Our ego has been described as a throwback from human evolution. It's the area of human consciousness that hasn't evolved from the basic animal instincts, or what some people call the 'reptilian brain'.

Just go to the zoo and take a look at the monkey cage to watch the ego in action. If you look closely you'll see a link between their behaviour and yours. The territorial squabbles, the selfish behaviour, the cliques, the sulking, the need for prestige and the fight for power. Do you notice yourself in there, in the monkey cage?

Monkey behaviour	Human behaviour
Territorial squabbles	Road rage
Cliques	'She's my friend, not yours.'
Mating behaviour	Saturday night in your town
Prestige	'Look at my new Mercedes.'
Dominance	Clawing your way up to the top in your company
Sulking	'Poor me, it's just not fair.'
Grabbing the bananas	Snatching all you can get out of this life

• ALONE IN A CROWDED ROOM •

Another way to look at our ego is to say that it separates you from other people and from what is missing in your life.

Have you ever felt alone in a crowded room? That's your ego telling you that you are separate from everyone else. It's the

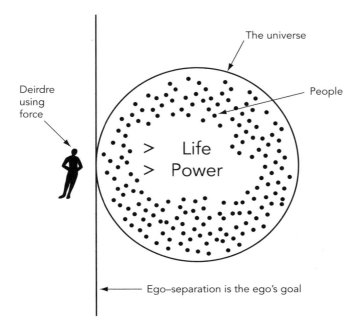

only roadblock between me and you, and you and the power that can help you become fulfilled.

Personally, my ego had me out there, by myself for 27 years, scrapping with life and all within it. Now that was very real as an *experience*, but it was not *reality*. I was victim to the age-old saying 'I'm an ego-maniac with an inferiority complex', forever comparing myself to others when the real truth was and still is that I'm no better or worse.

It's simple: if we want to be fulfilled and to regain our emotional health and sanity, we need to dismantle the power of our ego, which we know is protecting our warped instincts, so that we can be reconnected again with ourselves and with the world.

The problem we think we have (the superficial problem) is only a symptom of our real problem – which is 'living'. And for a living problems we need a living answer. And there isn't a living answer without giving up our ego. *And you can't give up your ego to you.*

Sometimes it's easy to justify our behaviour and delude ourselves, especially when it comes to protecting our basic instincts.

I can't sum it up better than the distinguished BBC correspondent Fergal Keane, in his memoir entitled *All of These People* (p. 344). Here Keane is describing a court scene where he was called to give evidence at the trial of a former Rwandan mayor who had organised the slaughter of 20,000 people during the 1994 genocide.

> Apart from that moment when I was asked to point him out, a dramatic flourish by Richard (the lawyer), I avoid looking at Gacumbitsi. I have seen enough of him. That confidence of his, whether it is real or constructed, makes me mad, and it makes me frightened. I don't know where he gets it from. I can't understand that you can do what he has done and look so at ease. The man is not a psychopath, a creature beyond the scope of logic or moral judgement. He is, or at least was, a Mass-going Catholic, a teacher, a man who went on official visits to foreign countries. That is the most unsettling aspect of this whole bloody business. He isn't from a separate species, or a candidate from the asylum. Gacumbitsi is a man who loves power. He is what becomes of us when we crave power above everything. His crimes came about because he believed the Tutsies of the RPF were going to take away that power.

'Isn't it extreme,' you may ask 'to exterminate men, women, children because you wanted to stay mayor of a nowhere municipality in a nowhere country?'

No. Not when the country has always resolved such issues by killing the minority. Not when you are brought up with such violence. Not also when the state from its highest levels orders the killing and prevents any investigation or conviction. And not when you regard that minority as vermin. You fear them so you kill them. You make a world without enemies. Gacumbitsi was no madman. He followed the logic of his time and place.

What is the logic of your time and place?

You know, like Gacumbitsi, but thankfully with less devastating consequences, we just go blindly on, accepting our struggle to survive, our fever for success, resentments, lack of time, regret of the past, fear of the future, and the worship of power and prestige.

I used to be really critical of people, places and things. I realise now that it was because I wanted unconsciously to build myself up. I was envious (often masked as interest) of people who lived what I thought were successful lives. And so I found myself thinking things like 'Oh, it's OK for her, her dad's incredibly wealthy' or 'He only got that job because he knew the owner', or 'She's attractive, but hasn't she got thick ankles!' I was always looking for faults in other people. I loved to tear people down because secretly it just made me feel better. Not you? Are you really sure?

See if you can find yourself in these examples below.

Everyday examples of being railroaded by the ego

Situation	Ego response
Debbie was walking her dog and came upon a neighbour with whom she normally chats. He turned away from her, because he felt embarrassed about the news that he'd been made redundant. Debbie felt hurt and angry and has avoided him ever since.	Debbie needs to be liked, and feels secure in herself when everyone treats her nicely. Her threatened social instinct made her angry at the neighbour because he seemed to reject her, when actually he had other reasons for turning away.
Paul, who lives in a busy neighbourhood, applied for planning permission to build three new homes in his back garden. He learned that his neighbour, David, objected to the plan because the neighbourhood was already congested. Paul responded by dragging his key down the side of David's car.	Paul had a long-time dream of buying a house in Spain with this added revenue. David's objection was a threat to Paul's emotional and material security, so Paul had to retaliate.
Emma is single and works in a small company. She had enjoyed being the only young attractive woman in the company, until Donna arrived. Emma secretly hates her.	Emma thinks that Donna, also single, is a threat to the relationships that she has with others in the office and that this new co-worker poses a threat to her sexual ambitions.
Pat called Janet to ask if she and her son could be included in the Beavers run. Janet said she would call her back, but with her busy schedule, she forgot.	By not getting the phone call from Janet, Pat thought that Janet and the other mothers were snubbing her. This was a threat to her personal relationship instinct.

Matt took Sharon out on a date and took her to his favourite restaurant. She didn't like it and asked to leave, so they had to walk out in front of the manager. Matt was fuming and said nothing to her for the rest of the evening.	Matt felt the need to put on a good evening for Sharon. Walking out of the restaurant was a threat to his pride, his self-esteem, his emotional security and sexual ambitions.
Richard sold his company, but was tied to the company as a consultant. He began to feel hurt that none of his former employees were returning his calls or respecting his advice.	No longer being the kingpin, Richard's pride, self-esteem and emotional security were affected because the satisfaction of these instincts was tied to his level of prestige and influence.
Nick's partner Julie made a sarcastic remark about their finances and his spending habits, and then wanted to have sex later that evening. Nick was having none of it.	Nick felt that Julie needed punishing for insulting him (i.e. affecting his self-esteem).

These are real people (with different names) with actual feelings and responses. Some of them seem justified, but most of them were appalled at their behaviour when they saw it in a different light. They learned that they are powerless over their instincts and egos.

It's like this: our minds are like computers, and our ego is a virus on the hard drive. If by ourselves we can't remove the virus, no matter how often we try to restart the computer, then to remove that virus, we'll need to take it to an expert.

And by this I don't mean a psychologist or therapist.

• PART 2: THE SOLUTION •

So what's the solution? How do we stop this happening? If you're just coming to terms with the idea that sometimes you are acting or reacting in a way that really isn't helping your goal of a happy, successful, fulfilled life, then you could be feeling pretty overwhelmed right now. Luckily the solution is very simple.

I'm not going to pussyfoot around this, so I'll be straight: to be free of what's blocking you from being fulfilled you need to believe in a power greater than yourself that can help you. That's the solution.

Anything else is bullshit. It won't work, it won't last, and I guarantee you'll keep revisiting the same old crap until you become willing to believe in something (it doesn't matter what) greater than you. Affirmations won't do it for you, a new partner, a new baby or a new job won't make you contented – nothing you can do by yourself is going to work.

But let's get something else straight and up front – *you don't have to believe in God*. But you do have to let go of the idea that you hold all the answers, and start being open to the idea of handing your problem over to a greater power.

> **Sometimes life is not about finding all the answers – it's about being comfortable with the questions.**
>
> Anonymous

The idea of handing your problem over is hardly revolutionary, because you do something similar all the time in your everyday life. In situations where you don't understand what's going on, or know you don't have the answer within you, you turn to an 'expert' – whether it's a doctor, lawyer, telephone engineer or mechanic.

In exactly the same way, you've just admitted that there are areas in your life that you don't understand, that you cannot personally fix, so why doesn't the same approach come as naturally with this, or with other life problems? We'll look at that in a moment, but most importantly. . .

- It doesn't matter what you believe in, or don't believe in.
- You don't need to 'get it' right now: I've been following this programme for nearly 20 years and I still don't get it – but I do know that it works.
- All you need to do now is keep an open mind to the possibility that there are things outside your understanding.

• START WHERE YOU ARE •

We need to start where we are on this journey. We can start from any point of belief or non-belief, and we don't need to have any religious or spiritual affiliation. And just to make it absolutely clear, I'm not asking you to believe in God. If you do, fine – if you don't, still fine. This programme will work regardless. But we are learning a whole new perception of your role in the universe. Cool, eh?

This reminds me of the story of my husband, Bryan, learning to drive in England. In his mid 30s Bryan moved from the US to the UK. He'd held a US driving licence for 20 years at this time, yet Bryan had many challenges and frustrations driving in England. First, he'd been used to automatic gears, and our car had a manual gearbox. He'd been used to driving on the right. The roads were much narrower here than in the US, parked cars seemed to be everywhere (making the roads even trickier), the rules were all different and to cap it all off, it was often raining or icy. Bryan failed the British driving test twice. He had to relearn everything, he needed to start from where he was, and feel that was OK. He passed the British driving test on his third attempt. Driving in a different way is just like living in a different way. You can start this very personal journey from whatever place you happen to be in, as long as you have the willingness to make a start.

• WILLINGNESS IS THE KEY •

There is a principle which is a bar against all information, which is proof against all arguments and which cannot fail to keep a man in everlasting ignorance – that principle is contempt prior to investigation.

Herbert Spencer, English philosopher

Coming to believe in a higher power is like the opening of a door that seems securely closed and locked. All we need is a key, and the decision to swing the door open. There is only one key, and it is called willingness. Once unlocked by willingness, the door opens almost by itself. Even if you can't be willing, why not try to be willing to be willing?

So please keep an open mind and a willingness to see the world in a different way. The mind that's looking for answers to life is like a person who is looking for something they've lost with a torch. If we hold the torch in one place we're never going to find what we're looking for. But if we move it around and look in nooks and crannies, we'll make progress.

But let's be honest: for many of us, the starting point here is one of scepticism about handing over problems to a 'higher power' – particularly if you don't happen to have any religious beliefs. You might say, *'What exactly am I handing over and who am I handing it over to, and most importantly, what's going to happen to me after I do it? Am I just going to be a doormat for the world to step on?'*

Now here's a mindblower: all this protesting is not coming from you. That sceptical voice is your ego desperately trying to hang onto its control of you. Because if it lets go, that means you're actually going to have to look at yourself and accept things about yourself, such as your neediness, your control, your instincts and defects – and that would be embarrassing. I'm here to tell you that it's not embarrassing – it is the *only* way to a freedom beyond your wildest dreams.

But for the analytical types, let's look at it from a scientific angle.

• WHAT DOES SCIENCE HAVE TO SAY • ABOUT A POWER GREATER THAN OURSELVES? (OR 'QUANTUM PHYSICS IN TWO EASY PARAGRAPHS'.)

There's an order to the universe. In the last 50 years, scientists have been looking at the universe in a whole new way. The universe, according to physicists, is a giant magnetic field, the power of which is beyond our imagination. Historically it was believed that the universe was chaotic, a mass of meaningless data and disorder. With computer technology scientists realised that there is indeed a pattern or an 'order' behind it all and that the universe is powerful, understandable and organised. (Unlike you and me!)

There is no such thing as 'objective reality'. Until the twentieth century, everything we thought we knew was based on a man in a white lab coat jotting down his Eureka! results from testing his hypotheses. Much of this research was based on causality: 'a this causing a that'. Enter Einstein, Heisenberg and their cronies. What they've shown us is that, as a scientist conducts certain experiments, *the very act of observing changes the results*. If this whets your appetite, you'll love the 'Double Slit Experiment'! Here, one scientist sees a different reality from another scientist. Other great brains from the quantum world put forward an argument that it is only the presence of conscious observers, in the form of ourselves, that makes the universe exist. If we take this to be true, then the universe only exists because we are looking at it. OK, my head is hurting and I guess yours might be too – it's understandable if you don't feel much desire to go deeper here, but suffice to say that science is now proving what mystics have been rabbiting on about for centuries: *each person bases their observations and their truths on their own perceptions of reality*.

• WHAT DOES THAT HAVE TO DO • WITH A HIGHER POWER?

It means that what you are observing in life is not objective (or what you think of as 'real' or provable) but it is all a subjective experience. In other words, your mind takes all the information that comes into your head and processes it so you can make sense of it. Take this book, for example, that you're holding in your hand. It seems like a solid substance, but it's actually made of tiny atoms, endlessly moving about. By the same token, your life history, stored in your mind, is affecting how you perceive and react to everything you do.

Now suppose this: what if there were something beyond your ordinary understanding, some unseen power, that might help you?

Wham! There shut the gates of our minds as we say: '*If I can't understand something, it can't be true.*'

Well, how about just for a while, you allow the possibility that you don't understand everything, or that *things can change just by suspending disbelief.* If you need some more 'grounded' examples of the power of thought then here are a few to get you started.

How about one man overturning a global empire? Mahatma Gandhi overpowered the British empire by simply believing and stating that the Indian nation should be free, and then peacefully mobilising a whole continent.

What about technology? The Wright brothers in the US were laughed at for believing they could build a machine that would fly. But due to persistence and focus, they made it happen. And fewer than 70 years later, men were walking on the moon.

Take a good look at nature, how marvellous and beautiful it is. Have you ever looked at something and been overwhelmed, temporarily lost for words at its perfection?

If you're having difficulty with this step, just remember the last time you had an 'overwhelmed' feeling and use that as your first step in believing that there might just be something more powerful than you, even if you don't know what it is or how it works.

• IT'S ALL UNFOLDING JUST AS IT • SHOULD – A HIGHER POWER IS AT WORK

I'd like you to think back over your life – and put away that violin, we're not going to play the victim any more (we've all done that long enough) and think of the major events in your life. If that's too tough, think back over the last five years. Write out all of the important events, both good and bad, from the earliest to the present. Be especially careful to focus on turning points, such as a new job, or starting university, significant relationships starting or ending and so on.

Date	Life event	Resulting life events
June 2005	I met Tom.	He inspired me to apply to university.
Nov 2005	I hated my course so I changed to food nutrition.	I met Jane, who introduced me to my current business partner.

Now see the pattern: think back, you may not have thought this at the time, but now you can see how the patchwork of your life to date has brought you to this point . If you can't see this now, at least accept that whatever has happened in the past has brought you to a place where you have got your hands on this book!

Another thing that might jump out is that you haven't been in total control during all these life events – some things happened because of events over which you had absolutely no control (we've all had moments where we stepped off the pavement and should have kissed that bus).

Many who are reading this and completing the exercise may think they are not happy or fulfilled, but the real truth is that you don't know what will make you fulfilled, you just think you do. You can dream of a new car, job or relationship, the fact is that you won't necessarily be happy with it. If you want to make personal fulfilment your goal then you need to 'give up' on the thought that you know what it will look like. It's impossible to know what will happen tomorrow, next week or next year and if you got what you thought you wanted now, then you may regret it as time moves on.

This is true of goal-setting, which has become hugely popular in recent years. Now I'm all for goal-setting, it does focus me on what I think I want to achieve, but I say this with a caveat. Setting goals is OK as long as you can handle both ends of the stick. So your goal may be to get a huge pay rise by the end of the year and if you get it you'll be happy. And if you don't? So perhaps it is better to set your goal as acceptance: acceptance of the outcome whether your goal has been successful or not. As the age-old prayer goes:

Grant me the serenity

To accept the things I cannot change

The courage to change the things I can

And the wisdom to know the difference.

OK, I'm jingling my key of willingness, so what do I do now with my ego?

Good question. First of all, learn to like the miserable bastard and just accept that it's within you.

Also, try to give up any idea of conquering the ego, because it's been controlling you since you were born. You can't use force on it, you will need a power greater than yourself to be free of its control.

• FIRST STEP. . . •

CHOOSE YOUR OWN HIGHER POWER.

That's right. . . you get to choose your own. If you have religious beliefs and that feels right, this could be straightforward. If however the idea of a higher power is a totally new concept, take some time to really think this through.

Get in a comfy place or take a nice walk while you're doing this. Now think of what you'd like your higher power to be like, what qualities it would have. Free yourself from any ideas of a stern, judgemental figure and think only of the good qualities. For example your higher power might be forgiving, patient, loving, kind or cheerful. Some people find that visualising a beautiful image helps – whether it's a mountain, a tree, or whatever. You can call your higher power anything you'd like. Or nothing at all. Whatever feels right to *you*.

• NEXT STEP. . . •

MAKE A DECISION TO LET GO OF YOUR EGO TO YOUR HIGHER POWER.

This is where we quit playing God in our lives. We accept that we aren't running the show any more, and decide to let go of our control over our life.

Aha, but what of my free will? Do I just give it all up, and stop believing I can create my own successful future, and doesn't that go against every other self-help and success principle? Not really. Your free will can either move along with this power or it can move away from it towards your ego. And as you've discovered, when you move towards your ego, your life is a struggle.

Make no mistake, this can be a terrifying step, especially if you're someone like me who likes to be in control. And I did wonder what was going to be left of me if I handed over my will. Would I be the same person? Would I be forced to join a monastery? Here's what actually happened after I let go of my control:

- I felt alive for the first time in my life and realised that I had a new strength arising out of complete defeat.
- I gained the courage to start a company with no experience or outside financial help.
- I learned to become a halfway decent leader of people.
- I was able to deal with personal tragedies and setbacks while remaining relatively calm.

Anybody who's met me – and I hope that you and I do meet one day – knows that I am no doormat.

Back in 1991 I had to have faith that this process would work. I now have the results that it does. It's like this: the exhaust is nearly falling off your car. Six months ago you took the same car to a local garage but they ripped you off. You don't trust them. So you ask a friend, do they know a good garage, and can they recommend one? You trust your friend and you believe in their judgement – anything's got to be better than the garage that's ripped you off before. You take the car into the garage and they do a great job: Good value, good service, and your exhaust looks OK. You now have proof that this garage can handle your car repairs and when something goes wrong with your car again, you're going to that same garage again – no question.

Close your eyes and ponder on that little story.

This is how you need to feel when you make your decision to have faith in something other than you. It's as if you're about to sign a contract for your personal happiness. This document will be as watertight as any experienced lawyer could draft. Your part in the deal is to follow the suggestions and have faith that the results will be more than you could have hoped for.

• TRY THIS •

We can take our first steps in doing this by selecting a short period of time in our day and, as Dr David Hawkins suggests, letting go of our 'positionality' as each moment arises. This means that each moment something happens, we let go of our position on it, so that *when something arises or someone says something, we decide not to take a position about it, but just let it happen.* You might try this and see what it feels like.

In whatever way works for you, you need to come to believe and accept that you are not in control, you are not the centre of the universe and that there is a power greater than you. Believe me, when you get to this place, everything is ready to get a whole lot better! You no longer feel alone and you don't feel the need to prove anything to anybody.

I realise that this may not make a bit of sense to you now, but trust me, it will. Remember this is an experiential programme, not a philosophical one. We only see the value of these steps after we've experienced them.

The power to help you become fulfilled will come from taking the action in the next three Steps (or chapters). Our whole purpose, now that we've got this far, must be to uncover and remove our personality defects (aka our ego), which have been caused by misdirected basic instincts. If you have decided to move ahead to unblock what has been causing you to be restless, irritable and discontented, then nothing short of rigorously honest action will bring about the change you want in your life.

Sometimes when we're at this stage we're like a mountain climber. Imagine that you're an inexperienced climber and you've got yourself into a fix on the side of a cliff. You're dangling at the end of a rope, hanging hundreds of feet in the air, and there's no way back up. Death is certain. Should you hang in there, or let go? Most people would say it's courageous to keep fighting, but Stan van Hooft, in his book *Life, Death and Subjectivity* (p. 197) suggests that holding onto something that doesn't work is like our futile attempts to control our lives:

> **It is the ignorance of one who sees within him- or herself the only source of meaning. I prefer a form of subjectivity that acknowledges its dependence upon the world and upon others. This is a form of subjectivity that does not**

> rely upon self-affirmation for its meaning. This is a form of subjectivity that acknowledges its place within larger realities such as society and the world of nature. It is part of a larger process and must on occasion fall into line with those processes. Its mortality and finitude will not be a curse to it. Such a subjectivity feels peace in the face of fate and acceptance in the face of death. Such a subjectivity can let go.

The choice is now yours: you can keep doing what you're doing, expecting different results. Or you can try a new way of doing something. Even better, just for today, try accepting that the universe manages the circumstances of your life; you live them. The universe is supplying the next moment; your job is to contribute.

• LETTER TO THE UNIVERSE •

I've found this technique works really well for some people. You've just selected a personal higher power, now tell it how you feel, what brought you to come to believe in something greater than you, and that you've made a decision to hand your ego/self-will over to 'it', and what you're hoping for. Nobody needs to see this, or know about it, but you and your higher power. Try it, it's a great start.

Dear _____

_____

_____

_____

_____

_____

STEP IN BRIEF

- All of your problems stem from trying to satisfy your basic instincts, which are protected by your ego.

- You can't fix yourself with yourself.

- Willingness is the key to gaining belief in a power greater than you.

Step Three

TAKING STOCK

• • •

And you will have knowledge of what is true, and that will make you free.

John 8:32

Now that we understand what our problem is, and are willing to decide on trying a new solution, it's time to take a series of *actions* to help us get there.

The first part of this Step is to analyse how our *thinking* has contributed to our problem. We call this taking an inventory. This is where the real work of this programme begins. And for some of us, it may be the first time we've taken a really honest look at ourselves and how our mind works – it's fascinating, challenging and exciting – but weird at first.

• • •

This Step is one of the most liberating and helpful exercises you can do for yourself – *ever*. If you do it honestly and unflinchingly, it will:

- free you of the resentments and fears that you've become used to living with;
- liberate you from being a victim, because now you see the truth about yourself;
- give you an understanding of why you act the way you do and feel the way you feel;
- help you to look the world in the eye;
- begin to give you a feeling of serenity and courage.

For perhaps the first time in your life, if done sincerely, this Step will help you feel happy, joyous and free. It's nothing short of brilliant. On a personal level, this is the action that set me on the path to real success because it helped me to be rid of my fears and resentments and know who I am.

• WHY IS THIS STEP CRUCIAL? •

Until now, this book has been only a mental preparation for you to take action. We've seen that you've been living on a lifetime's dose of misdirected instincts protected by your ego, and our ego doesn't like us to look at these defects. Why? Because it's too painful or embarrassing. You can't admit them, even to yourself. Done properly, this is not a quick look in the mirror; it's an MRI scan of your character.

What if you don't do this step? In the world of AA, alcoholics who don't take this step frequently go back to drinking (and claim that AA doesn't work!) because returning to the bottle is the only way that they can cope with their obsessions and emotional baggage. Your case may not be as extreme as that, but *you will experience no permanent effect without honestly and fearlessly completing this step.*

JUST DO IT!

Put a sock in your ego's mouth and commit to doing this exercise. It has been my experience that it doesn't really matter what your attitude is, or whether you believe this will work or not. What really matters here is that you follow the instructions and complete the Step honestly and to the best of your ability.

• YOUR PERSONAL INVENTORY •

GETTING IT DOWN ON PAPER

A quick and easy way that you can deal with resentments and, fears and harms done to others and yourself is by listing them and then trying to look at your part in the issue. If you want lasting results, though, it's best to analyse them properly. Analysis generally means recording and sifting through for the truth. So, if you're really serious about personal change, I urge you to complete the exercises in this chapter.

We'll begin by analysing how our minds work with *four written personal inventories*. This will help you to assemble the truth about yourself, which lets you work through the rest of the programme.

We'll look at your:

> *resentments* – people or places that you think have harmed you in some way, causing you to feel bitter;
>
> *fears* – what you fear or worry about in the past, present or future;
>
> *sexual conduct* – how you may have misused this most basic instinct;
>
> *harms you've done to others* – actions that you have taken that may have hurt others, including yourself.

I say 'written' because you must put it down on paper to look at it objectively. It's the writing down that triggers the release. If this information stays in your head your ego will do its best to change it, justify your old thinking and eventually forget what you've learned. So you have to write it down.

To help us in this, we'll be using some practical forms written by spiritual teacher Joe McQuany that will make it simple. After you read this chapter you can download and print these off from thepersonalrevolution.net. Or you can complete them online and save them in your personal vault.

• THIS ISN'T ANY OLD • FLAT-PACK PROJECT

There are generally two types of people when it comes to taking instructions:

1 Those who follow them meticulously, step by step. You know, the type who get everything out of the IKEA box, count out the screws and the Allen keys and work through each numbered step.

2 And those who groan when they see the IKEA diagram and packets of screws and just start building with scant regard for the instructions; those who are then baffled as to why they have built a table with three legs!

As we're talking about something far more important than DIY furniture here, that is, your life, then be the nit-picker for once. If you take the time and effort to follow these directions carefully, then the end result for you will be much more effective.

• TAKING AN INVENTORY OF ME LTD •

Suppose your mind is a company and suppose you had no idea what you had to sell, or what you needed? You wouldn't be able to meet the needs of your customers. You'd have a lot of stuff you couldn't sell taking up shelf space. You would soon go bust, right? Well, you're about to take stock of your mind to prevent yourself from heading towards emotional bankruptcy.

So what are you trading today?

Who are the squatters who are living in your mind, rent-free?

What are you giving away?

Who's sabotaging you?

Most importantly: *What's rotten, unsaleable and taking up space in your head?*

Answer: Your out-of-control basic instincts, which – because of your ego – have become *character defects.*

• OUR STOCK-IN-TRADE •

Let's look again at these instincts and see what's gone wrong to cause us to feel restless, irritable and discontented. Looking at them as something entirely natural, we can understand that these instincts serve a good purpose. They are the emotional and psychological make-up of being human and are necessary for our survival as individuals and as a species. For example, fear on a healthy level keeps us in check; without any fear we would live recklessly and dangerously. Anger on a balanced level is also good, as it can drive us to set boundaries with other people about what's acceptable to us.

But we know, as we've read in Step 2, that these instincts can become warped in almost all of us, especially when we try to force our will upon others. The more bent out of shape these instincts are, the unhappier we become.

The founder of the 12 Step programme, Bill Wilson, describes our human condition so well in the book *Alcoholics Anonymous.* Read this a couple of times with an honest and open mind:

> **The first requirement is that we be convinced that any life run on self-will can hardly be a success. On that basis we are almost always in collision with something or somebody even though our motives may be good. Most**

people try to live by self-propulsion. Each person is like an actor who wants to run the whole show; is forever trying to arrange the lights, the ballet, the scenery and the rest of the players his own way. If his arrangements would only stay put, if only people would do as he wished, the show would be great. Everybody, including himself, would be pleased. Life would be wonderful. In trying to make these arrangements our actor may sometimes by quite virtuous. He may be kind, considerate, patient, generous; even modest and self-sacrificing. On the other hand he may be mean, egotistical, selfish and dishonest. But, as with most humans, he is more likely to have varied traits.

What usually happens? The show doesn't come off very well. He begins to think life doesn't treat him right. He decides to exert himself more. He becomes, on the next occasion, still more demanding or gracious as the case may be. Still the play doesn't suit him. Admitting he may be somewhat at fault, he is sure that other people are more to blame. He becomes angry, indignant, self-pitying. What is his basic trouble? Is he not really a self-seeker even when trying to be kind? Is he not a victim of the delusion that he can wrest satisfaction and happiness out of this world if he only manages well? Is it not evident to all the rest of the players that these are the things that he wants? And do not his actions make each of them wish to retaliate, snatching all that they can get out of the show? (pp. 60–1)

Did you identify with any of that? Now close your eyes if you don't think you can swallow the next paragraph:

> are not most of us concerned with ourselves, our resentments, or our self-pity? Selfishness – self-centredness! That, we think, is the root of our troubles. Driven by a hundred forms of fear, self-delusion, self-seeking and self-pity, we step on the toes of our fellows and they retaliate. Sometimes they hurt us, seemingly without provocation, but we invariably find that at some time in the past we have made decisions based on self which later placed us in a position to be hurt... So our troubles, we think, are basically of our own making. (p. 62)

This is the truth that your ego doesn't want you to see. Personally I remember that someone lent me the book *Alcoholics Anonymous* when I was in Japan all those years ago. The book itself is around 600 pages and when I dropped it on my bed it fell open at this passage. It was the first time in my life that I had read the truth about me, and it really did make me think that if someone can describe me so well, then maybe they knew how to help me get out of this unfulfilled and miserable existence I was living.

Coming back to the idea of an inventory, a business will see it as a fact-finding, fact-facing, truthful exercise. Anything less and the effort is wasted. Your personal inventory is similar:

Business inventory	*vs*	*Your inventory*
fact-finding		searching
fact-facing		fearless
truthful		moral

To succeed you need to be fearless in your search for the truth about yourself and your reactions to what has happened to you so far. You are going to search out and put down on paper those things that are painful, embarrassing, which fill you with shame or fear or any other uncomfortable feelings – the stuff that you wince at, thinking, 'Oh God, not that!' This will include your resentments, fears and harms that you've done to others and yourself. If you're thinking, 'I don't need anything this drastic', then remind yourself, or I'll remind you, of why you picked up this book in the first place – you can't be totally happy with your world. Keep that lovely mind of yours open.

When we take stock of ourselves it means we own our actions, we did it to ourselves, or it was done to us. So our inventory belongs to us and us alone. To be fair, it is essential to find a high level of motivation for this as it would be all too easy to say 'I don't need to do this' or 'What's the point, I'm not that bad' or 'I'm different.' Come on now, are you really? It's like this: when was the last time you went to bed at night hopping mad or embarrassed about something that happened during the day and you still had an emotional hangover from it the next morning because, surprisingly, those feelings didn't disappear overnight? How old are you now? 20, 30, 40, 50? That means you've got a lot of those days sitting in the filing cabinet in your mind. Most never need to see the light of day, but others need the dust blowing off them and shredding.

I promise you, this spring clean of your mind is possibly the biggest favour you could do for yourself. Your world will be an altogether better place as a result. You might not see how at the moment, but trust me, it will change your life. And it's well worth a bit of initial discomfort.

So, the four main areas where we need to be searching and fearless are our *resentments, fears, sexual conduct and harms done to others and ourselves.* Almost all negative issues you have on a day-to-day basis can be placed under one of these headings: you are either mad about something, or afraid of something or someone, or you've done something to someone else or yourself that causes you to feel remorseful. Most of these will be current issues; however, if you can stomach it you may want to go further back to your childhood or adolescence for a thorough clear out.

resentments = *wrong* judgements

fears = *wrong* believing

harms done to others = *wrong* actions.

• LET'S KICK OFF WITH THE NUMBER • ONE OFFENDER: RESENTMENT

So, what is resentment? Well let's look at the Latin root of the word with the prefix *re*, and *sentire*, which means 'to feel'. So, it's to re-feel a wrongdoing. If you think that someone or something has done you wrong then you replay that feeling of bitterness, indignation or anger in your mind like an old record that's stuck. As if that's not bad enough, you then take a perverted delight in not only thinking about it but telling others about it. Oh, don't we all love that feeling of righteous indignation, especially as our friends and family often join the *'No way!'* – *'He said what?'* – *'How dare she!'* – Party. Every time you tell the story of the wrong-doing, you 're-feel' it and, although you're trying to get it off your chest, it just doesn't go away, in fact it feels even worse, and to cap it all you get a sick sort of satisfaction out of your victimhood.

I hear you; you're thinking '*That's not me!*' Well if it wasn't, if you didn't feed off the juice that your resentment is giving you, then you'd just let the wrongdoer out of your head, and the resentment would go. But you can't, can you? Why not? Because as long as you can cast them as the villain, it means you don't have to look at your part, and that will protect your self-esteem. The resentment sits there like a big squatter in your mind, refusing to budge; in fact it just gets bigger as you keep rethinking and retelling the tale.

• SELF-PITY: RESENTMENT • AGAINST OURSELVES

Once you have been hurt or offended by another person, some-times you can then just have a resentment about your lot in life – with the '*It's just not fair*' attitude to life. This self-resentment is nearly always linked to those people against whom you have a grudge. Think about it: when you turn your anger and resent-ments towards other people, you 're-feel' what that person has done to you and those 'feelings' often turn inwards, leading to unhappiness, apathy and disappointment. If you do this (or you may know others who are skilled at feeling self-pity and talking about it!), then you're in for a rough ride as you'll be a total reactor with your fulfilment always at the whim of how others live their life and their response to you.

• A RESENTMENT BUFFET •

Sometimes it's hard to uncover our resentments – or even think that we have any. But I've found that, once I popped the lid, I was amazed at how many there were. I've had the great privilege to be a guide for others and they've made the same discovery.

Here are some examples from people I have known to show you what I mean and maybe help you see some of your own:

From adulthood

I'm resentful at:

My father: he wouldn't lend me the money for a new car.

My boss: she overlooked me for promotion.

My work colleague: he got the promotion and I'll need to report to him now.

My company: the owners are stingy and won't give me a pay rise.

My stepfather: he got ownership of my mother's property when she died – it should have gone to me.

My children: they haven't achieved anything in life.

My employee: she's taking advantage of the system.

My wife: she's lazy and won't get a job.

My mistress: she told my wife about our affair.

My husband: he never spends time with the family.

My neighbour: he plays loud music at 2am.

My best friend: she's got it all, husband, kids, lifestyle.

My childhood friend: she didn't invite me to her wedding.

The Labour Party: they just followed the Americans and went to war in Iraq.

The NHS: I have to wait six months for my operation.

Thin women: they must be happier than me.

From adolescence

I'm resentful at:

My father: he always compared me to my older brother.

My father: he criticised me constantly.

My father: I never saw him, he was either working or on the golf course.

My mother: she was a religious nut.

My mother: she controlled me and pushed me into subjects I didn't want to do.

My parents: they were poor and I couldn't get the stuff everyone else had.

My parents: they divorced and there were constant arguments.

My first girlfriend: she jilted me and told me I was a loser, especially in bed.

My first boyfriend: he told his friends about our sex life.

My school: the teachers were unprofessional and didn't care enough.

From childhood:

I'm resentful at:

My mother: because I was adopted.

My mother: she worked and I had to walk home from school alone.

My mother: she told me that she wanted a boy and she got me.

My mother: she always pushed me to achieve and was never satisfied.

My father: he left us when I was 4.

My father: he was a Muslim and I went to a Catholic school.

My father: he lost his job because he was an alcoholic.

My father: he always got new jobs in different areas and I had to change friends often.

My brothers: they used to hit me.

My uncle: he looked at me lustfully.

My primary school teacher: because he told me I was stupid.

My classmates: because they called me 'specky four eyes' and 'fatso'.

God: because he allowed my sister to die when she was 8.

Most people think that you can deal with resentment by forgiving someone. That may work for saints, but not for you and me. A far more effective way is to see our part in it. This is why taking an inventory of our resentments is a groundbreaking way to examine this damaging area of your life.

• RESENTMENT SURGERY •

Let's take one resentment and analyse it. We'll use the one mentioned on p. 32. Remember Paul's resentment at David's objection to Paul's planning permission application?

WHO AM I RESENTFUL AT?

- **Paul has resentment against David.**
  We write down the person who has done something to us.
  It might be your boss, because he didn't give you the promotion that you wanted, or your friend who didn't invite
  you to her wedding, or your partner for a multitude of
  reasons. It's the person (or organisation, or even principle)
  that caused the wrong that sits at the forefront of your
  mind, eating away at your time and energy. This is why you
  start by listing the person's name.

WHAT IS THE CAUSE?

- **David objected to my planning permission.**
  Take a look at why you are mad at them, that is, what they
  have done to you.

WHAT BASIC INSTINCT HAS BEEN AFFECTED?

- **Paul's emotional and material security – because he
  might not have the revenue to build his house in
  Spain.**
  Here take a look at the basic instincts that have been
  harmed. As you've seen, basic instincts make us human,
  but they also make us resentful when one of them are
  stepped on. You might need to go back and refer to the list
  of basic instincts on p. 19.

Now, if we stop here, we can conclude that this world and its
people are often quite wrong, and that they will continue to
wrong us – so we have a right to be resentful. If we harbour
those thoughts, they will end up dominating our minds, causing

us to give our thoughts and power over to the people and things that we resent. You are actually giving them power over you! Do you really want to carry on doing this? When this happens, it scuppers the decision that you've just made in Step 2. This means that you will never have access to the necessary power to bring about a change in your life, because you are handing over your power to those that you think have harmed you.

So let's look at the resentment again and add another part, the most important part – that is, the part that *we* played in the situation.

WHERE HAVE I BEEN INCONSIDERATE, DISHONEST, SELFISH, SELF-SEEKING OR FRIGHTENED?

- **Paul had been *inconsiderate* because he didn't stop to think what his addition would do to the neighbourhood; *self-seeking and selfish* because he only cared about getting the extra revenue; and *frightened* because he feared that his dream home had now vanished.**

This part may be hard to swallow, because this gets to the real truth about you, and it's a completely different way of looking at your life. To date, you've been living it on the basis of protecting your misdirected basic instincts. When you live your life like this, you spend your time and energy, consciously or unconsciously, protecting these instincts with your ego. Which means you get angry, fearful and do stuff that harms or hurts others and, hey presto, they retaliate! Remember the quote from Bill Wilson earlier in the chapter? I'll remind you:

'we invariably find that at some time in the past we have made decisions based on self which later placed us in a position to be hurt... So our troubles, we think, are basically of our own making.'

If you can begin to see it this way, a whole new truth about your life is opening up for you. You'll begin to understand and accept that it was you that actually caused the other person to react the way they did. *'But hang on a minute, there's plenty that people have done to me that I had no control over,'* I hear you say. You're right, but even holding onto old resentments where you have done nothing to cause them is *your* responsibility also, and you'll discover a way here to let them go. Personal growth is not about pinpointing someone else's issues, only your own. I know it's hard to believe, it was for me too, but this is the truth.

The final part of our inventory is the key, because whether you are looking at a resentment, fear, sexual conduct or a harm you've done to another, the fundamental cause of it is the same: *somewhere along the line you've shown a lack of consideration, been dishonest, self-seeking or selfish or you've been fearful.* You may not be able to see this at first but you'll be shown how to spot these character defects when you write your inventory. To help you along, here are some examples of these character defects in action; there are plenty more:

- **Inconsiderate**: Here we show little regard for the rights and feelings of others. For example, ignoring someone at the office because we are too focused and busy, or not playing with our children or listening to our partner, or spending far more on stuff than we can afford, resulting in others going without things. Being inconsiderate may also imply that we didn't give time to understand the complete truth about something (e.g. we might be upset that someone jumps the queue at the doctor's surgery, until we realise that the person had a toddler who was waiting in the car).

- **Dishonest**: This can range from downright lying and stealing to padding our expense account, taking a sick day from work when we are not sick, not taking the blame for something that was our fault – even pinning the blame on another, or looking at facts in a twisted manner to suit us.

- **Self-seeking**: This is when we have a secret agenda and are motivated to manipulate others for our own selfish ends. This can be as simple as only helping others to enhance our prestige (rather than for totally selfless reasons), sabotaging a colleague's chances of promotion, or using sex as a means to get what we want. Self-seeking agendas rise to glory in the world of business and sadly this is why you, I and many other people get frustrated with our work and colleagues and tragically can't understand why.

- **Selfish**: This is blatant behaviour that's aimed at protection of Number 1. We've got something and we want to keep it, or we want to get something, and we disregard others. Time is an obvious one here. How many of us are selfish with our precious time?

- **Fear**: Many of our troubles arise out of self-centred fear. We're afraid that we won't get our basic needs met for security, society or sex.

To sum up:

Action 1	Action 2	Action 3	Action 4
I am resentful at:	The cause:	Affects my:	Where have I been:
People, places and things with whom I am angry.	I ask myself, what did they do to me to cause this anger?	Which basic instinct has been affected? Has my self-esteem, my security ambitions or sexual relations been harmed or interfered with?	*Selfish *Dishonest *Self-Seeking and frightened *Inconsiderate? Which of the above defects played a part in creating this resentment in the first place?

• INVENTORY 1: REVIEW OF • RESENTMENTS

In the following table, Joe McQuany has arranged the aspects of a resentment that we've been talking about in a four-column grid (reprinted with the permission of the Kelly Foundation).

The beauty of this kind of written inventory is that you don't have to analyse this information part by part as the inventory process will do that for you.

This system works for analysing your resentments, fears, sexual conduct and harms done to others.

Review of our Resentments

		'SELF' COLUMN 3 — Affects my... (Which part of self caused the resentment?)								COLUMN 4 — What is the exact nature of my wrongs, faults, mistakes, defects, shortcomings:			
		Social instinct		Security instinct		Sex instinct		Ambitions						
COLUMN 1 — I'm resentful at:	COLUMN 2 — The cause:	Self-esteem	Relationships	Material	Emotional	Acceptable sex relations	Hidden sex relations	Social	Security	Sexual	Selfish	Dishonest	Self-Seeking/Frightened	Inconsiderate
1														
2														
3														

IMPORTANT POINT: Instead of following your instinct to write from left to right, it is crucial to complete the columns one at a time going down. This saves you from having to change your mindset four times as you complete them. It also depersonalises the process and helps you to focus on the facts.

HOW TO COMPLETE THE INVENTORY SHEET

Action 1

(NB Complete column 1 from top to bottom. Do nothing on columns 2, 3 or 4 until column 1 is complete.)

List the names of all the people, institutions or values that you believe have wronged you. This is all you do. Just list the names, in other words, you are naming the resentments by identifying them with the names of people or institutions. Remember you are doing this because it's generally the person that you're mad at, even though it's what they have done that has harmed you. This should be pretty straightforward.

Action 2

(NB Complete column 2 from top to bottom. Do nothing on columns 3 or 4 until column 2 is complete.)

List all of the harms on your grudge list that these people, places and things have done to you. Write this down one at a time. This should be simple enough.

Action 3

(NB Complete each column within column 3 going from top to bottom, starting with the self-esteem column and finishing with the sexual ambitions column. Do nothing on column 4 until column 3 is complete.)

On your grudge list put a tick in each square that names your injuries. Was it your self-esteem, your security, your ambitions, your personal and sexual relations that had been interfered with? By this stage, you don't need to think any further about column 1, because the person or thing that caused this harm is irrelevant, done properly you should now be interested only in what instinct has been threatened in you.

Action 4

Putting out of your mind the wrongs others have done, look only for your own mistakes. Where have you been selfish, dishonest, self-seeking, and frightened, and inconsiderate?

(Asking yourself the above questions, complete each column within column 4.)

Action 5

Reading from left to right you can now see the resentment, (column 1), the cause (column 2), the part of self that had been affected (column 3), and the exact nature of the character defect within you that allowed the resentment to surface and block you from being happy (column 4).

A closer look at column 4

Because column 4 is a new concept and is so crucial to your quest to become fulfilled, let's take a closer look at some examples.

Listing one resentment from each area of the examples opposite, here is how we might look at our part in column 4.

Review of our Resentments

COLUMN 1	COLUMN 2	COLUMN 3 Affects my... (Which part of self caused the resentment?)									COLUMN 4 What is the exact nature of my wrongs, faults, mistakes, defects, shortcomings?			
		Social instinct		Security instinct		Sex instinct		Ambitions						
I'm resentful at:	The cause:	Self-esteem	Personal relationships	Material	Emotional	Acceptable sex relations	Hidden sex relations	Social	Security	Sexual	Selfish	Dishonest	Self-seeking/frightened	Inconsiderate
1 My company	The owners are stingy and won't give me a pay rise.	✓	✓	✓	✓				✓		✓		✓	✓
2 My best friend	She's got it all: husband, kids, lifestyle.	✓	✓	✓	✓	✓		✓	✓	✓	✓	✓	✓	✓
3 My father	Always moved around when I was young and I changed friends often. It was difficult and I was miserable.	✓	✓		✓			✓	✓		✓		✓	✓

1 *My company: the owners are stingy and won't give me a pay rise*

Generally companies reward dedicated workers; there could be many reasons why they haven't rewarded you. Three main ones could be:

a) you are not seen as an employee that is earmarked for a pay rise;

b) the company is struggling;

c) the owners or shareholders want to receive as much profit as possible.

So, if it's:

a) Then you're being self-seeking and frightened, perhaps expecting something for nothing. Are you really an exemplary employee?

b) Then you're being inconsiderate as the company just can't afford it, and surely it's reasonable to expect the company to be prudent during difficult times – otherwise many people could be out of a job.

c) You're being self-seeking (self-pity) and frightened as you want more of the pie that doesn't belong to you, or you are inconsiderate – why shouldn't the owners reap the rewards? They own it. Would you share the interest earned on your bank account with friends or neighbours if you didn't need to?

2 *My best friend: she's got it all: husband, kids, lifestyle*

Looking at your part in it, what you're experiencing is self-pity. You're wasting valuable energy wishing for what you haven't got, instead of being grateful for what's in your life, and even happy for your friend. She probably has no idea about your smouldering resentment and would hope (as

friends do) that you're there for her in good times and bad.
So, you're selfish inasmuch as you don't really care about
her well-being, you only care about yourself. You're dishonest, perhaps you secretly enjoy listening to the
problems in her life instead of empathising. You're self-
seeking and frightened, fearful that you won't get that
supposed great life that you think she has and, finally,
you're inconsiderate, instead of being a good friend (and
let's face it, good friends are hard to come by), you've
nursed a huge resentment against her. Ouch! It's painful to
see the truth (but ultimately it will make you a better
friend).

3 *My father: because he always got new jobs in different
areas and I had to change friends often. It was difficult
and I was miserable.*
Here's a childhood resentment that you would seemingly have
no control over and therefore would not be able to see your part
in the harm done to you. You can easily recognise the instincts
that have been interfered with, but I guess you're saying, '*How
could I be selfish, self-seeking and frightened, dishonest or inconsiderate? I was only nine.*' True, nine when it happened, but you're
not nine now. Look at it through your adult eyes, and not as a
hurt child. For whatever reason your father moved (and
remember this is your inventory, not his). Is your hurt not due
to self-seeking and fearful motives, just because you wanted to
stay in a certain area? He had his future and family to think
about. At the end of the day, aren't you just being inconsiderate, to expect people to change their world for you, just
because you were a 9-year-old when it happened? So I guess
you'd tick the self-seeking and frightened and inconsiderate
box here.

You may think that you have very few resentments, or that you have none at all. We all have resentments; it is the very nature of being human. But it doesn't matter what the other person did to you or how twisted he or she is. Your job now is to look at where you were at fault. Even when you don't think that you have done anything to cause this resentment, you can always look hard at your inconsiderateness as a last resort, which just means that you need to consider everyone's point of view. When you take responsibility, you regain control of your life.

I'd prefer it if it were my fault – then I can do something about it.

Things will continue to happen to you, just like the referee in a football match who gets kicked. But with this process under your belt you can dismantle them and look only for your part. Even when you can't see how it could possibly be anything to do with you, there's a tactic. Remember what you have learned about your ego and character defects operating to protect bent basic instincts? Well, don't think that you are unique. There is a whole planet of us doing the same thing. So here's what you do: the next time someone really offends or hurts you, remember that they are also struggling, and trying to make sense of it all. Think of it like this: if you went to see a friend who was physically ill in hospital and they were grouchy and rude, you'd show tolerance and patience and forgive them, wouldn't you? Then try to show the same tolerance and pity when someone hurts or harms you. There is now no reason to retaliate; you've seen where it's got you in the past. So there is no escaping the fact that your problems have to be your problems, and baby, you are the only solution.

Real Life Story

66 Here's the real life story of Sally, who is the carer for her disabled mother. She has two brothers who do very little to help. For years she has followed the age-old formula for failure: trying to please everyone. She has been resentful about her caring role for some time and finally snapped and took out her years of frustration on her brothers in a hurtful way.

Sally had the courage to look at this deep resentment against her brothers. She agreed that she had been self-seeking and frightened as she started off wanting everyone in her family to see what a caring and selfless person she was. Sally also saw that she was frightened of two things: asking her family for help (as it seemed to her a sign of weakness), and of the response she might get. Sally finally accepted that she was inconsiderate, expecting too much of her brothers when they were clearly unable or unwilling to give as she was giving. 99

• INVENTORY 2: REVIEW OF FEARS •

What's been keeping you stuck in a rut? Have you been waiting for the right opportunity to present itself before you make a move? It's natural and normal to want to improve yourself in some areas, but sadly many of us want to go from here to there without putting in much effort. And it's not because we're lazy; no, it's generally something much simpler than that. Along with all its derivatives, *fear* is the main culprit. Ask yourself how many times you've procrastinated over something because you're afraid that you can't or won't be able to do it well. If you can't relate to this then what exactly are you frightened of? Stick around; you might be surprised to find out.

Simply put, fear is an emotional response to threat or danger. It is a basic survival mechanism – the old reptilian brain within us operating in its 'fight or flight' mode. So there is a much-needed place for fear as part of our survival.

It doesn't end there though, and Bill Wilson sums up how fear has caused us constant problems:

> This short word somehow touches every aspect of our lives. It is an evil and corroding thread; the fabric of our existence was shot through with it. It set in motion trains of circumstances which brought us misfortune we felt we didn't deserve. But did not we, ourselves, set the ball rolling?'

Alcoholics Anonymous, p.67.

So what forms does fear take? Loads, and I'll list a few here:

Agitation, angst, anxiety, aversion, cold feet, concern, cowardice, despair, distress, doubt, dread, foreboding, fright, horror, jitters, misgiving, panic, phobia, procrastination, suspicion, terror, timidity, trembling, trepidation, unease, worry. . . add some more if you can think of them. But there's no need, as naming the type of fear is unhelpful. You now know that we react the way we do because one (or all) of our instincts has been threatened, and it doesn't matter if that threat is real or imagined.

So in this second inventory, it's your job to analyse your fears and see that most are imagined. If resentments are wrong judgements then *fears are a result of wrong believing*. Freedom from fear is a lifetime's job, but you can make a start by attempting to understand what you fear and also what others fear. Only then can you look your fears squarely in the eye and try to find a way to transcend them. I've read that the most effective way to deal with fear is to have faith – a firm belief in a friendly universe, in a world that makes sense, even though we can't see it at present.

You know, I'm a big worrier. I have always worried – Am I going to lose my job? Does my boss really rate me? Will my long-term boyfriend leave me? (he did by the way, for someone else, but I don't have resentment!). Did the saleswoman like me? Can I afford the mortgage? When will I die? Is this scab on my leg cancer? On and on and on. What a waste of life. How many of you worry about stuff that you really can't control and frankly have no place worrying about?

Let's get rid of it all, shall we?

1 You're going to look at who or what you fear.
2 Then you'll turn your attention to the cause of the fear, by asking what they or it are going to do to you; for example, are you going to lose or not get something materially, will it result in divorce, destroy a personal relationship, could you not get the job or lose your job or lose face?
3 You'll then look at which instinct has been threatened.
4 Then of course you'll look at your part in it, asking yourself which character defect caused you to hold onto the fear.

Returning to our life stage list, to keep it simple I've concentrated on current fears, as many of our childhood fears have morphed into our day-to-day issues in adulthood or have been forgotten about. Here are some examples:

Adulthood:

Being alone: I want to settle down and have children.

The bank: paying off my mortgage, or my house may be repossessed.

My health: it seems to be deteriorating.

My wife: she may get bored with me and leave.

My children: they may not get the grades I want for them.

My job: I may not get the promotion I deserve.

My job: I've padded my expense account for years.

My student debt: it's growing and I'm afraid of the future; will I be able to pay it off?

My friend: She's very opinionated and I don't think she likes me; she'll persuade the others that I'm not worth knowing.

My neighbours: I need to keep up appearances in case they find out who I really am.

My car: It's four years old and things will start to go wrong with it that I can't afford to fix.

Adolescence

My parents: I always had bad dreams about their death.

Girls: they used to call me ugly, so I was afraid to make friends.

The neighbourhood bully: I was afraid to go out into the road when he was there.

PE: I never took part in competitions, because I was afraid I would lose.

HOW TO COMPLETE THE INVENTORY SHEET: ONE COLUMN AT A TIME

Action 1

(NB Complete column 1 from top to bottom. Do nothing on columns 2, 3 or 4 until column 1 is complete).

List the people, institutions or principles of which you are fearful.

Action 2

(NB Complete column 2 from top to bottom. Do nothing on columns 3 or 4 until column 2 is complete.)

Ask yourself why you have that fear.

Action 3

(NB Complete each column within column 3 going from top to bottom, starting with the self-esteem column and finishing with the sexual ambitions column. Do nothing on column 4 until column 3 is complete.)

What part of self caused the fear? Is it your self-esteem, your security, your ambitions, your personal and sexual relations that have been, or may be, interfered with?

Action 4

Putting out of your mind what may or may not happen or has happened, determinedly look for your own issues and mistakes. Where have you been selfish, dishonest, self-seeking, and frightened and inconsiderate?

(Asking yourself the above questions, complete each column within column 4.)

Action 5

Reading from left to right you now see the fear (column 1), the cause (column 2), the part of self that had been affected (column 3), and the exact nature of the defect within you that allowed the fear to surface and block you from being fulfilled (column 4).

Review of our Fears

'SELF'

| | COLUMN 1 | COLUMN 2 | COLUMN 3 — Affects my... (Which part of self caused the fear?) | | | | | | | | | COLUMN 4 — What is the exact nature of my wrongs, faults, mistakes, defects, shortcomings? | | | |
| | | | Social instinct | | Security instinct | | Sex instinct | | Ambitions | | | | | | |
	I'm fearful of:	Why do I have the fear?	Self-esteem	Relationships	Material	Emotional	Acceptable sex relations	Hidden sex relations	Social	Security	Sexual	Selfish	Dishonest	Self-Seeking/Frightened	Inconsiderate
1	Being alone	I don't want to spend the rest of my life alone. I want to settle down and have children.	✓	✓			✓		✓	✓	✓			✓	
2	Losing my job	I've been padding my expense account and if my boss finds out I'll be fired.	✓	✓	✓	✓			✓	✓		✓	✓	✓	✓

Referring to your list again, let's take a look at a couple of examples to analyse:

1 *Being alone*:
   This affects our social and emotional instinct and ambitions. Most people desire companionship and don't want to see themselves growing old on their own. Looking at your part in this situation can help identify why you are alone. Perhaps you are truly career-minded and are therefore selfish with your time. Maybe you are the type that oozes self-pity and negativity, and your self-seeking and fear of rejection are apparent to anyone you come across, so they give you a wide berth thinking that you are not interested in them!

2 *Losing my* job:
   I've padded my expense account for years and may lose it. With the exception of the sex instinct, this affects almost all instincts. No matter how poorly you are paid, or that everyone else does it, or that your employer is stingy and deserves it, this is wrong. You know it is, and it's causing fear in you and this feeling will always block you from being fulfilled. End of story.

   Here's a real life story:

   " Fiona divorced her husband seven years ago. She has two children. After seven years of very little contact her ex-husband moved into the village where Fiona lives. He wants lots of access to their children and is constantly phoning the house. This has been going on for six months and Fiona is terrified that her young teenage children will soon prefer to spend time with their father rather than with her.

This fear was gnawing away at Fiona and served only to make her both miserable and moody, which was affecting her relationship with her children. So she looked at the root of it. She accepted that she was being selfish not wanting her children to see their father, indeed she acknowledged that it was not her happiness but rather her children's joy that she should be concerned about. She could see that she had been dishonest with her children by making excuses as to why they couldn't see their father. She was self-seeking and frightened – she had brought this fear on herself because she needed approval from her children. Most of all, though, she accepted that she had been totally inconsiderate towards everybody, including herself. "

• INVENTORY 3: REVIEW OF •
SEXUAL CONDUCT

Many of us may need an overhaul here. One of the deepest ways that we can harm or hurt people, including ourselves, is through sex: how we use it, who we use it with, when we use it. In this inventory, we are going to review this as it's the last area where we can finally be free of the baggage that's preventing us from moving forward. This is often where people wince and cringe with embarrassment but you've got to get this out. It's the final hurdle, you're very nearly there, and trust me, there's probably very little on this inventory sheet that hasn't also been done by your neighbour. You're not unique in this respect.

In *Alcoholics Anonymous* (on p. 69, would you believe it) Bill Wilson says:

We reviewed our own conduct over the years past.
Where had we been selfish, dishonest, or inconsiderate?
Whom had we hurt? Did we unjustifiably arouse

jealousy, suspicion or bitterness? Were we at fault, what should we have done instead?

Let's get this down on paper:

1 Cast your mind back to whom you have hurt, including hurting yourself.
2 Then write down what you did to cause this harm to yourself and others.
3 Looking at the basic instincts, identify which part of self caused you to do what you did. The social instinct, the security instinct or the sex instinct?
4 And then, column four: which character defect caused you to do this?

You should be flying through these inventory sheets now, but once again, here are a couple of examples to help you on your way:

Adulthood:

My wife: I flirt with other women to make her jealous.

My husband: I refuse to have sex with him – I don't find him attractive.

My husband: I refuse to have sex with him – I think I'm fat and ugly.

Myself: I go on sexcapades because I'm lonely.

Myself: I've had sex with two people in the office.

My work colleague's wife: one of the people in the office (above) is married.

One-night stands: I use men/women for sex and can't wait to get away the next day.

My ex: I always go back to him/her when there's no one else on the scene.

My friend: I let things go too far and led him/her to believe there was more than just friendship on the cards, even though I knew I didn't truly feel that way about them.

My friend: I dated his girlfriend and she left him for me.

Adolescence:

My girlfriend: I cheated on her constantly.

My mother: I became pregnant at 16.

Myself: I thought masturbation was wrong.

HOW TO COMPLETE THE INVENTORY SHEET: STILL ONE COLUMN AT A TIME

Action 1

(NB Complete column 1 from top to bottom. Do nothing on columns 2, 3 or 4 until column 1 is complete.)

List the people you have harmed.

Action 2

(NB Complete column 2 from top to bottom. Do nothing on columns 3 or 4 until column 2 is complete.)

Ask yourself what you did.

Action 3

(NB Complete each column within column 3 going from top to bottom, starting with the self-esteem column and finishing with the sexual ambitions column. Do nothing on column 4 until column 3 is complete.)

Was it your self-esteem, your security, your ambitions, your personal and sexual relations that had been interfered with?

Action 4

Putting out of your mind the wrongs others have done, determinedly look for your own mistakes. Where have you been selfish, dishonest, self-seeking, and frightened and inconsiderate? (Asking yourself the above questions, complete each column within column 4.)

Action 5

Reading from left to right you can now see the harm (column 1), what you did (column 2), the part of self that caused the harm (column 3), and the exact nature of the defect within you that allowed the harm to surface and block you (column 4).

Referring to this list, here is an analysis of a couple of examples:

1   *I've hurt my work colleague's wife (although she may not know about the brief affair), because I had sex with her husband*:
    Look at the columns and see the basic instincts that have been affected. Moving to column 4, let's look at the exact nature of your wrong. See if you can guess.

2   *I've hurt my mother because I got pregnant as a teenager and I feel guilty because she had such high hopes for me*:
    This affects the basic instincts across the board: social, security, sexual and ambitions. If you feel this way, then look at your part. Do you agree that you may have been selfish, doing only what you wanted to do without consideration for others? Oh, so you've been inconsiderate; perhaps you've also been self-seeking, depending on the circumstances (maybe you really got pregnant to get away from your parents and get your independence).

Review of our Sex Conduct

	COLUMN 1	COLUMN 2	'SELF' COLUMN 3									COLUMN 4			
			Affects my... (Which part of self caused the harm?)									What is the <u>exact nature</u> of my wrongs, faults, mistakes, defects, shortcomings?			
			Social instinct		Security instinct		Sex instinct		Ambitions						
	Who did I harm?	What did I do?	Self-esteem	Relationships	Material	Emotional	Acceptable sex relations	Hidden sex relations	Social	Security	Sexual	Selfish	Dishonest	Self-Seeking/ Frightened	Inconsiderate
1	My work colleague's wife	I had sex with her husband.	✓	✓			✓	✓	✓	✓	✓	✓	✓	✓	✓
2	My mother	I became pregnant at 16.	✓	✓		✓		✓	✓		✓	✓	✓	✓	✓
3															

Real Life Story

66 Just before I went to work in Japan I hooked up with a really nice guy who told me that he had very strong feelings for me. Secretly I didn't care one way or another about him as I was about to start a new life abroad. I was honest and let him know that I was leaving to work in Japan in a few months, but kept him hopeful that there might be some long-term future as I wanted the emotional security of a relationship and didn't want to be alone. For about 18 months after I left on my world trip, I kept on reeling him in whenever I felt lonely, giving him false hope again.

This little story of how I had deliberately harmed another person was on my sex conduct sheet. Looking at the final columns here's what I found: I was totally selfish, concerned solely with *my* needs, plans and desires. I was dishonest with him, letting him think that there was more to this relationship than there was. I was self-seeking and frightened, only staying with him because I was afraid of being alone and of course I was totally inconsiderate. 99

• INVENTORY 4: REVIEW OF HARMS • DONE TO OTHERS

Besides harms caused when pursuing the 'basic instinct', there are bound to be other cases where you've stepped on the toes of others. These are the episodes that keep us looking over our shoulder instead of living peacefully in the present. Your final list will be the harms and hurts you have done to others, including yourself – *you'll find that few people have hurt you as much as you've hurt yourself.* Some harms will come from the sex inventory, others from your fears and resentments inventory. In fact, I think you'll find that you've hurt many of those people and institutions listed on your resentment list more than they have harmed you. Some of these people may be weighing heavily on your mind (whether you realise it or not), so come on, let's finish off with inventory number four.

HOW TO COMPLETE THE INVENTORY SHEET, LISTING FROM TOP TO BOTTOM

Action 1

Whom or what did you harm?

Action 2

List what you did.

Action 3

What part of self caused this?

Action 4

What character defect was involved?

Action 5

Reading from left to right, you now see the harm (column 1), the cause (column 2), the part of self that had been affected (column 3), and the exact nature of the defect within you that allowed the harm to surface and block you (column 4).

This whole process requires an open mind, as wide open as you can get yours. Often you'll find that these defects are deep within you, buried under thick layers of self-justification and sick rationalisation that relieves you of the guilt and remorse.

Review of our Harms

	COLUMN 1 Who did I harm?	COLUMN 2 What did I do?	'SELF' COLUMN 3 Affects my... (Which part of self caused the harm?)									COLUMN 4 What is the exact nature of my wrongs, faults, mistakes, defects, shortcomings:			
			Social instinct		Security instinct		Sex instinct		Ambitions						
			Self-esteem	Relationships	Material	Emotional	Acceptable sex relations	Hidden sex relations	Social	Security	Sexual	Selfish	Dishonest	Self-Seeking/Frightened	Inconsiderate
1	My employer	Padded my expense account.	✓		✓				✓	✓		✓	✓	✓	✓
2	The pre-Japan boyfriend	Kept him hopeful of a long-term relationship and used him.	✓	✓	✓	✓	✓	✓	✓			✓	✓	✓	✓

With this in mind, thoroughness ought to be the watchword when taking your inventory.

• TIPS •

To make this challenging step as easy as possible, here are a few simple suggestions to help you start the process.

- Have a good supply of inventory sheets – at least four of each.
- Get your favourite pen – you don't need to erase or edit anything as nobody other than you, and perhaps your guide, will see it.
- Have a notebook handy with you at all times to jot down anything that comes to mind (and I mean anything).
- Get a ring binder to put your completed sheets in – best to put them in chronological order with the most recent events first. There is no specific reason to do this other than it's a practical system.
- Find a comfy place to write in – one where you feel relaxed. Close your eyes and ask for the courage and willingness. In other words, it's not advisable to race in from work, sit down at the kitchen table whilst people are cooking the dinner; or sit on the 7.50 a.m. train, slurping back your latte trying to think of who harmed you! No, be gentle with yourself. This is a major task that you are about to embark on so give yourself space and time to complete it.
- Remember to complete the columns one column at a time. This depersonalises the process and helps you analyse the facts.

- Write, just write. It doesn't have to be perfect – just get into the habit of writing. Start by writing what comes up – get it down on your sheets – even if you don't think it is relevant – it doesn't matter, just write – and the rest will come. Morning times are often a good time to write – so set your alarm early and start this process.

- Write every day until your inventory is complete – if you don't do this consistently you won't complete it. Commit to at least half an hour a day.

- Keep to the facts. What *exactly* happened or what *exactly* are you afraid of? You may have many opinions and feelings about events and fears – but these are not the facts. *What you think doesn't really mean much. Thoughts are not things.*

- Be responsible for the privacy of your inventory. It may help if you transfer it to your personal page on www.thepersonalrevolution.net for safe keeping. Then there is no way anyone other than you can see it – which therefore gives you no excuse not to write it all down. Don't think in your mind that you had better not write this or that down in case someone claps eyes on it – nobody will, so don't leave anything out.

- If it suits you, you can complete your inventory online and save or submit it to your virtual guide.

- Finally, if you get 'blocked', remember that 'blocked' is just in your head and is not reality. I'm no writer, and if I gave in every time I was blocked, I would still be on the Introduction to this book! Make a commitment to move forward by taking action or, if it helps, look for inspiration and like-minded people on www.thepersonalrevolution.net. More than anything, do it for you.

PART 2: SHARING YOUR PERSONAL INVENTORY

We are born free – free from what anyone else does. And we give that up ourselves by buying into things, by giving other people resentments, and fearing this, and worrying about that, and developing these selfish, self-seeking parts of our character. And then we end up confined by alcohol or food or other people (or other compulsive behaviour), and this all gets wrapped into a great big ball, a cobweb of emotional tangle.'

McQuany, J. *The Steps We Took* (1990), (p. 83)

By untangling the cobweb, this next phase of this Step will give you some of the most rewarding feelings of the entire programme. I realise that doesn't make sense, but in this process we do not know the results of a Step until after it's taken. In this Step your previous decision to let go to your higher power and the effort and honesty of your inventory become meaningful because we begin to get some results. *Personality change begins only as a result of doing this step.* Why? Because by sharing our inventory with a trusted person we begin to acquire a proper form of humility. I don't mean humiliation – that's definitely not what we're talking about – but it is what most think of by 'humility' (remember, if you've made it this far, you have vast amounts of courage and integrity).

Humility means that we begin to see and live with our true self. It means that we're teachable. You've got the ability now to stop performing the double act you've been rehearsing for years. Hasn't it been exhausting?! No longer do you need to be the character that you believe society thinks you should be. Now you have the opportunity to be yourself in a way you haven't been since you were 2 years old. You're getting very close to being the star of your own show.

So what is involved with this phase? Well, when you have all four sections of your inventory completed, try to set aside a block of time to talk this over with a person whom you trust and who is not *emotionally* involved in your life. This person can be a counsellor, a trusted friend, a member of the clergy or a virtual guide (who can even be anonymous) on www.thepersonalrevolution.net.

• WHY DO I HAVE TO REVEAL ALL • OF THIS?

Let me give you four good reasons:

1 **You can't really trust yourself to see the truth**

You might say, '*I've actually learned a lot about the traps and inner workings of my mind, so I'll just go ahead on my own from here.*' Let me just remind you that if you've had a resentment or other problem for weeks, months, or even years, and didn't even know you had a problem, it's pretty obvious that you're not an expert on the truth!

Remember back in Step 2 when quantum physics showed us that each human being has their own perception of the truth? It's like the witnesses of an accident on the street. Each person will tell the police a different story – depending on their emotional involvement. Well, it's safe to say that your emotional involvement in your fears and resentments has given you a distorted opinion of the truth, so it's best to get an objective view.

Particularly with resentments, you'll need a second opinion. You have conned yourself about the truth for so many years, can you really trust yourself to know what's right? Even if you're being as honest as you can, how honest *is* that at this point? You have to get someone who's not emotionally involved.

2 **You will be cheating yourself of opportunities for a better life**

Here's an example of this in action. I was helping a woman who, for one reason or another, hadn't worked for about 12 months. She had a 10-year-old son. On her fears list she had 'computer course', which she wanted to start but was afraid to, because she said that she was too stupid to learn computer skills.

Working across the instincts, she understood which ones were being threatened. Now, when she faced the fourth column she could only accept her defect as 'fear' and couldn't see any other during her self-analysis. After much discussion and debate, she accepted that she just *'Didn't like computers, didn't want to take the course and liked staying at home'*.

Looking more closely, I was able to help her see that she was both *selfish* and *inconsiderate* in that she didn't take her personal advancement seriously enough. Why? Because these skills, she agreed, would give her advanced employment opportunities and help her and her son have a better quality of life.

Seen in this light, she realised that her fears were bogeymen – and needless to say, she's on the course. What might be holding you back from being fulfilled? You'll only learn it by completing this step.

3 **It will save you heartaches in the future**

It was after taking part in this liberating process that I began to see and understand exactly who I was, what I liked, what I was good at, who I was afraid of, who I needed to avoid and who I needed to stay close to, my jealousies, my anger, my anxieties and dashed dreams and know that *I was responsible for all of it*. No more wallowing in self-pity, fear, guilt or remorse. With this new-found knowledge I couldn't help but change and accept life on life's terms.

The columns have become an integral part of my life: I've learned that I can't do anything about other people (what's in columns 1 and 2). I can't do much about self (column 3), except make a decision to turn my instincts over to my higher power – so from then on it's HP's business. The only thing that's my business is column 4, now those I can work on! And when I do, my personality is transformed. And this transformation is what will take you to a more fulfilled life.

4 **It will make you free**

Once you have taken this step you will really know what personal freedom means and how to shake off the bondage of your past. I remember being so embarrassed and fearful taking this step with my guide, a tough woman called Joyce from Manchester. After she'd finished helping me through the process, I stopped regretting my past and only saw my part in it. I remember it as if it were yesterday. In one instance, during a long drawn-out 'poor me' discussion about one of my resentments, which centred around redirected mail from a lover who had jilted me, she looked at me wearily and said, '*Deirdre, this happened seven years ago, you've got to get this crap out of your head and move on*' and only by using the directions and the process of the inventory was I able to give an eviction notice to the person who'd been living rent-free in my head for years. That resentment of seven years went away in five seconds.

• CHOOSING YOUR GUIDE •

Free yourself from finding the perfect guide. As Joe McQuany said:

> 'Although we want to have confidence in the person who hears our inventory, there's really no great wisdom or insight necessary on his or her part. I remember someone came up to me and related a situation in great detail. And it was obvious to me as soon as I heard it what the problem was. I said, "This is your problem right here." The person looked at me and said, "How did you know that?" "Well, you told me," I said. "How could you see it so plainly?" the person asked. And I answered, "I wasn't involved in it; you were."'

SO WHAT SHOULD I ASK MY GUIDE TO DO?

1   To make it easy for them, you should first give them a copy of 'Fulfilled Notes for Guides' (this can be downloaded from www.thepersonalrevolution.net or found in Appendix 3). It summarises what you've learned about instincts and

character defects, so that you and your guide will be using the same language.

2　Then sit down with them, take a deep breath, put a sock in your ego's mouth and cover the information across each of the rows.

3　This is not a confession, so there's no need to wail, moan or whip yourself. You're not reciting a list of your sins; you're looking for the *exact* nature of your wrongs. So with each resentment, fear or harm your focus should be on column 4. Don't spend too much time on columns 1 and 2, because that will give your ego ample time to interrupt and rationalise your wrongs. You are looking for *your* part, not the other person's.

4　This will be intense, so after an hour take a five-minute break to clear your mind.

5　Trust your guide. In most cases, they can easily see the real truth of the situation.

Do it online

For simplicity and ease, you can do this all online – anonymously. Complete the inventory charts, submit them to an anonymous guide and get immediate feedback via instant messaging on www.thepersonalrevolution.net.

Take a few moments and really make a commitment to yourself that you're going to follow this through. So many beautiful things will follow. After I took this step, I think the biggest discovery was that my intense ache of isolation had vanished, and I felt (maybe for the first time) that feeling at ease with the world was now a real possibility.

So, get your pen and paper and begin!

STEP IN BRIEF

- To become fulfilled you need to clear what's been blocking you.

- The main blocks are:

  resentments = wrong judgements

  fears = wrong believing

  harms to others = wrong actions.

- Sharing your inventory helps you to get an accurate picture of the part you've played in your life to date.

Step Four

CHANGE IS THE NAME OF THE GAME

• • •

The longer I live, the more I realize the impact of attitude on life. We cannot change our past ... we cannot change the fact that people will act in a certain way. We cannot change the inevitable. The only thing we can do is play on the one string we have, and that is our attitude. I am convinced that life is 10% what happens to me and 90% of how I react to it.

Charles R. Swindoll, American author and Clergyman

Changing your life for the better is not really about getting or adding – for the most part it is based on what you are prepared to give up. Now that we know what our shortcomings are, we need to find a way to eliminate these defective thoughts that have affected the way we think and live.

In this step you'll learn how to recognise and give up your old ways of thinking and behaving, allowing room for a new set of principles for living to enter your life. Done willingly, this is where the results of the programme will start to show.

• • •

All of the steps you've taken so far have been the preparation ground for taking this step. We've looked at the problem in Step 1, the solution in Step 2; we analysed the truth about our character, ego and defects in Step 3 – now we're ready to start changing.

So Step 4 is about letting go. It's about giving up those defects of your character that have blocked you from being fulfilled. It's about change and it's about you and your life, which is about to get much better.

Well, as ever, there is no gain without pain and we've still got some work to do. This step is based around the age-old principle of 'practice' and we get good at what we practice.

It is our attitude at the beginning of a difficult undertaking which, more than anything else, will determine its successful outcome.

William James

The hardest part about practising something is getting started. Take my daily run for example. I really used to dislike running – thought it was too much like hard work, especially in the north of England where there's often a harsh wind combined with icy rain. But after having my second child, Ava, I just couldn't shift the baby weight. A colleague was in the same position as me and she was singing the praises of how running is such a time-efficient and effective exercise. She looked great, and OK I'll admit I was envious, but I took action so I can forgive myself! One morning I put my old training shoes on and tried, walking at first, with a bit of jogging. A couple of days later I gave it another go. I was breathless and really didn't enjoy it. I couldn't see what all the fuss was about; I mean who would get excited about this joyless activity? It beat me; I hated the thought of it. But you see, I so wanted this baby weight off me, I persisted and pushed myself to jog just that little bit further each day. Within about a month I was running 5–6 km easily. It was just like going out for a walk. It wasn't difficult; I'd practised it so much that daily exercise has now become hardwired into my brain. People sometimes say to me, 'Wow, you run and exercise every day, that seems like hard work.' But you see it isn't, the starting of it was difficult, but now it's just something that I do without thinking about it. It's like brushing my teeth.

And this is where we want to get to with our character defects. We will need to practise giving them up. If that sounds like a killjoy, remember the rule of physics coined by Aristotle, who said that 'Nature abhors a vacuum'. And it does: if you give up a character defect, then something else will replace it.

Self–will	Good-will
When we are controlled by our ego, we are:	With change we become:
dishonest	honest
selfish	generous
self-seeking	humble
frightened	courageous
inconsiderate	considerate, compassionate
intolerant	tolerant

• THE LONG AND THE SHORT OF IT •

A shortcoming is an attribute that we are short on. What this Step centres around is taking those shortcomings that you identified in Step 3 (e.g. selfishness, impatience, pride and being inconsiderate, amongst many others, which are all children of the ego) and becoming willing to have the humility to let them go. This does not mean that they will vanish from you miraculously (there's no way of getting rid of our ego entirely), so the best that we can hope for is improvement little by little. Of course this is difficult, as so many of us hang onto our character defects and shortcomings because we've spent a lifetime crafting them. They are like our security blanket, they are all we know.

This reminds me of a story I was told about how spider monkeys, which are considered to be a delicacy in parts of the world, get captured. These monkeys are notorious for being very fast and difficult to catch. The locals however came up with a cunning plan when they realised that spider monkeys loved fruit. So they make small holes in a tree and place the fruit inside its trunk. The monkeys just can't resist and as they make a fist to grab the fruit they get stuck in the hole in the tree. In swoop the local hunters in full view of the monkey, but does the monkey move? No, he can't, because he won't let go of the fruit, which is in his hand. He is then easy prey for the hunters, because it never occurs to him that he can save his life simply by letting go.

• THE TRUTH ABOUT OUR DAILY LIVES •

How many of us have woken up in the morning in a bad mood about what happened the day before? And carried that emotion or feeling into the day? You think you're in control of your life, just as the spider monkey does no doubt, but your fears and resentments are controlling you. You have to learn to let them go otherwise you will continue to be controlled by your instincts and you'll be back where you were at Step 1.

You are the author of your own character defects, they've been with you since childhood and they affect your reality. You probably think that you are acting and reacting moment by moment, but actually you are replaying history with well-worn strategies and techniques for dealing with events. Personally I'm wired to have financial insecurity; it's been with me since I can remember. Now even with the wealth that I've created I'm still afraid I'll lose it all – why is that? Well, it's because it's still real for me – even though it's a lie. So I've created my own character defect. I can now see it (from the Steps, but especially Step 3) and therefore I can be personally responsible for my behaviour, emotions and attitudes. No one else is responsible, only me.

Now you've gathered the evidence to prove that many of your old ideas are wrong – and this may be the first time you've ever done that in your life.

You might now be thinking, well, if I give up all of these defects, who am I going to be? Am I going to be too good to enjoy life, am I going to have any fun? Am I going to be a doormat? Not at all – I'm no doormat and have done pretty well in all areas of my life, including starting and building a multi-million pound business, which doesn't happen if you're somebody who can be pushed around.

• SO WHAT MAKES US READY • TO CHANGE?

What makes you go to the dentist when you have a toothache? You don't want the pain any more; you give up and go to the higher power (who in this case happens to be the dentist). The very same analogy applies to your life. You've seen that these defects are objectionable to you, and how they are blocking you from being truly happy. Now, you can choose to do one of two things with this information:

1 **Keep doing the same old stuff**
   You can keep on doing the things that you are doing; the thought of the effort of change being too much. Your feelings may be painful, but at least you are familiar with them. Who knows, you may secretly enjoy hanging onto your old self. I mean, who doesn't like to feel self-righteous and indignant? Who wants to give up gossiping? And there's no doubt – we really do get a strange satisfaction from envying others – either for what they have or who they are. We

spend far too much time wishing we were different or envying those who have what we want. But if we learn to see that envy, resentment and putting down others are actually all making us feel miserable, then isn't it worth at least experimenting with giving them up to see what difference it makes?

2 **Start to make a personal change**
If you believe that the results (the benefits) of change could far outweigh your fear of changing (i.e. you have more to gain than you have to lose), and you begin to change your inner reactions to problems 'out there', then you start to deal with issues as a rational adult rather than an emotional adolescent. Here are a few examples from my life to illustrate this:

- In my early 30s I was busy running my business, but still wanted a relationship. Full of fear and self-pity, I was always on the lookout for a partner. In fact the thought often consumed me. It was only when I surrendered this and thought, 'What the hell, if it happens it happens', but with an inner knowing that it would happen, that I met my wonderful husband Bryan around two months later. You see, I let it go and the result in the change of my behaviour brought Bryan and me together. I wasn't desperate and needy, I just let it happen.
  Emotion/Attitude: neediness, self-pity, control
  Alternative rational action: let it go, accept powerlessness
- Running my company, I was often faced with difficult situations, and the most challenging involved working with my staff – they were following their basic instincts

just like me. However, I learned pretty quickly that if a staff member wasn't working out it was best to act on this early and not procrastinate for fear of morale issues and people thinking that I was too harsh. Once I took the decision to let a person go, without fail, everything was better for everyone.

Emotion/Attitude: fear, resentment, self-seeking

Alternative rational action: courage, selflessness

- I have deep-seated financial insecurity. When Bryan first came to the UK I lived in an old cottage with no central heating. I could afford to have it installed, but I was perfectly comfy with my hot water bottle. However Bryan, a Texan, found it hard going. One cold morning, when he could see his breath in the air when shaving, he gave me an ultimatum: 'We either buy central heating or I'm leaving.' So I had to let go of my fear of financial insecurity and get some radiators put in!

Emotion/Attitude: fear, inconsideration, stubbornness

Alternative rational action: acceptance, show consideration

- Some time ago I became involved in a potentially huge litigation dispute. This was one of the most difficult periods in my whole life. In the worst-case scenario, my family would still be OK financially, but I was terrified, and my fear had badly warped nearly all my basic instincts. I remember sitting with my lawyer trying to out-think and outmanoeuvre the other side. One day I brought a whole host of potential scenarios to my lawyer's office, 'What if they do this, what if they think that, they could go for this, God what if they find that?' – my worry list was endless. My solicitor – a very smart man – let me blather on, and then said: 'Look, we can only work on what is in front of us and not get distracted by what may be thrown at us. It's a waste of energy and you'll go insane, and you may even take me with you.' I had to hand the whole problem over to him, trust his advice and have utter faith that it would work out. Of course it did in the end, as things do. With hindsight, I can't believe how much time I wasted fuelled by self-centred fear during this period – *fear* (and we can spell this out as false events appearing real) that I would lose what I had and not get what I want. **Emotion/Attitude**: fear, resentment, control **Alternative rational action**: courage, let it go, accept powerlessness

So, we can choose to respond to life in the old way by reacting to our emotions or in a new way by taking rational actions, and trust me, rational actions are much more effective in helping us on our path to fulfilment.

In my company, when emotions were flaring between individuals, my mantra was always '*Let's put principles before personalities.*' In other words, not who is right, but what is right. This was a much more effective way to live and work in society than the unmanageability I had when running life on my feelings. This was how I began to live, trying to do the next right thing, one day at a time. The results of this philosophy for me have been nothing short of astonishing. They can be for you too.

• OK, SO I'M READY, WHAT NEXT? •

The key to making this step work in your life is attitude. Just as willingness was necessary to making a start on the previous Steps, that same open-minded and willing attitude is needed to begin this life-changing phase. Step 4 isn't a quick fix; it's a continual process of discovering and removing what is objectionable to you and then allowing something better to come into your life.

A wonderful illustration of why 'removing' or 'giving up' or 'handing over' your shortcomings is so important is offered by the internationally renowned author and speaker in the field of self-development, Dr Wayne Dyer, in his book *The Power of Intention*. Here he gives seven steps for overcoming your ego's hold on you.

1 **Give up being sensitive and easily offended**. It's your choice how you react or don't react. The easiest way to lose your contentment is to allow another person or thing to have power over you. In effect you are making them your higher power.

2 **Give up your need to win**. Believe me, the drug of achievement is temporary and addictive . It's impossible to win every time, and when you don't win, the result is frustration, resentment and shame.

3 **Give up your need to be right**. When you allow yourself the right to be wrong, it's just freeing, because you no longer have to prove anything to anybody. Amazingly, rather than people using it against you, this 'olive branch' encourages them to give up their need to be right as well.

4 **Give up your need to be superior**. What? Not you? Well, the next time you're enjoying a good gossip, check your

motives. Are you trying to build yourself up by tearing someone down? And the energy you use to hold someone down keeps you down there as well. Give it up.

5 **Give up the chase for more.** Happiness is an inside job. What exactly are you going to do with a bigger house anyway? Fill it with more stuff? Letting your ego write your wish list will always leave you unsatisfied. Instead, have faith that your needs will always be fulfilled.

6 **Give up identifying yourself on the basis of your achievements.** Ever heard of Henry Irving? A hundred years ago he was the most famous actor in the world. A hundred years from now, there will be all new people on this earth and no one will remember your achievements. I like the enlightened stance of musician Frank Zappa, who said: 'I don't give a f*** if they remember me at all.'

7 **Give up your reputation.** As we've seen with quantum physics, everyone's perception of the truth is different, so how can you control the thoughts of others? As my guide Joyce has said: '*It's not what they think of me that matters, it's what I think of them.*' In other words, *it's not a case of thinking less about yourself, but thinking about yourself – less.*

I have a lovely story about this last advice regarding reputation. This was my first experience of the power of having my ego crushed. I was still living in Tokyo and had become friendly with a modern-day monk from Boston whose name was Ray. I met Ray for our weekly coffee and chat and he noticed immediately that I seemed preoccupied and asked me what the matter was. I told him that I'd made a fool of myself flirting with a guy and it was really bothering me. Ray listened and asked, 'When did this happen?' I told him it was about a week ago. He said,

'Let me ask you a question: when someone says something inappropriate to you, how long do you think about it?' I replied that I didn't give much thought to it, really, perhaps a few minutes if that. Ray said, 'If that's the case, then why do you think you are so important that he would be thinking about *you* for a week?' These were some of the most profound words I had ever heard. They effectively kicked me out of the centre of the universe, and I've never forgotten them.

I learned to let go of my reputation, and with letting go I learned to take risks, and by taking risks I learned the secret of fulfilment: *give up, discover, discard and trust in the power of the universe.* Before this knowledge came to me I was operating through sheer brute force, fuelled by self-will. Finally I was beginning to understand that wallowing around in self-pity, hoping that things may work out for me eventually was never going to happen. I sensed however that with this programme of change under my belt great things were possible. I also accepted that I was the master of this new-found information and I had a choice: either be a prisoner of my ego or invited to join a whole new way of living.

• START PEELING THOSE ONION LAYERS •

You know, you're not really depriving yourself of anything here. When you harness the power of letting go of your shortcomings, the 'stuff' that you need will be provided – it has to be; we've already seen that there is no possible vacuum in this life. You can't get rid of a defect; it gets filled automatically with something better.

Just like deciding to lose weight for example. If you want to change your body image you need to do something differently.

Your body is the result of the food you put in, just as your mind is the result of the thoughts you put into it every day. If your body image has become objectionable to you, you change the things you eat: no more cakes, chocolate and fried food. You have to eat something though, so you chomp away at healthy food, which more often than not is green, washed down with the odd sneaky treat. The results are obvious to all. You like your new image, your self-esteem goes up and so eating healthily becomes a habit. This isn't easy though, is it? It takes continued effort to keep the weight off. How many of us do well on a diet for the first month or so and then slip back into our old ways?

It's the same with your objectionable thoughts, you don't like what they are making you feel or do. A flip of a thought can happen in a second, saving you hours, even weeks of negativity. So you need to spot your old ways of thinking and behaving, and say to yourself, '*This is objectionable and I know where it leads me.*'

The process then would be:

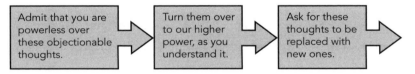

| Admit that you are powerless over these objectionable thoughts. | Turn them over to our higher power, as you understand it. | Ask for these thoughts to be replaced with new ones. |

In this way, we start practising new behaviours: patience, tolerance, compassion and love. At this point you might be thinking: '*Why do we need our higher power again? Can't we just cut out the middleman, and make a conscious decision to be more patient?*' Try it and see. But from my experience, if we do that we will be using force instead of power, and we'll be back where we started with Step 1.

If the mind acrobatics don't do it for you then try this: the next time you're angry say, '*I'm angry, but I'm willing not to be*' or '*I'm afraid, but I'm willing to look at it another way.*' This offers a sweetener for your current feelings and can take away the immediate jagged edges of your issue. Now you know the truth – which is that you have a choice in how you react to things and you can learn to react to things differently. In AA they talk about acting 'as if', meaning you can really act how you want to act and be who you want to be. Perhaps now is the perfect time to recreate some aspects of your personality.

This new way of behaviour does take practice – lots of it. We'll never do it perfectly, but the result will be obvious to all – more people will enter your life and more opportunity will come your way. You'll grow in courage, feel free to take risks, be connected with the world around you. Surprisingly your life will just get better, it just will – it has to, because you're not the same, and if you're not the same the world around you won't be the same either. Just as Dr Wayne Dyer says, 'Change the ways you look at things and the things you look at will change'.

Step 4 takes self-awareness, which you now have after taking Step 3. It also needs effort and action. Like an archaeologist, your job is to dig around for the truth. And just as the archaeologist needs patience in digging for their treasures, you'll need to be patient, knowing that these lessons will be revealed according to your ability to handle them, and not according to how quickly your ego thinks you should!

• TRY THIS •

From what you learned in Step 3, list your character defects as you understand them. In the opposite column focus on what positive quality you'd ideally like it to be filled with.

Defects I want to 'give up'	Qualities I want to work towards
Examples:	Examples:
Pride	Humility
Greed/overeating	Restraint
1 _____	_____
2 _____	_____
3 _____	_____
4 _____	_____
5 _____	_____
6 _____	_____
7 _____	_____
8 _____	_____
9 _____	_____
10 _____	_____

• SPOTTING YOUR PERSONAL • WARNING SIGNS

Here's a great exercise that you can try for a 21-day period to help you know when your character defects are popping up. It focuses on your external behaviour, which acts as a barometer to your internal thoughts and feelings. Adapted from something called The Personal Craziness Inventory in Dr Patrick Carnes's book, *A Gentle Path through the Twelve Steps*, this exercise will help you look at your routine behaviours and spot where they are unbalanced in your life. Following that through, you can generally recognise which defect of character has caused this behaviour and make a start on removing it.

1 **Physical well-being**: There's an old saying: 'Your health is your wealth.' So how's yours? Are you getting regular exercise (or over-exercising), eating junk food, being a coach potato, getting too much or too little sleep? Do you dread the cold and flu season because you know you're going to get it? When do you know that you are not taking care of your body? List two examples.

_____

_____

2 **Getting around**: Are you regularly late for the train or the bus? How many points on your driving licence? Any road rage incidents (even just pounding the steering wheel or shouting in your car)? Take a look at the floor of your car – are you growing any mushrooms? When was the last time your car was serviced? List two examples of these behaviours that show that your life is getting out of control.

_____

_____

3 **Living space**: Not spending enough time on your personal household tasks and errands is an indication of your inability to manage. You know, laundry piled up, an old bit of cheese in the fridge, dishes unwashed, the cat-litter box

unchanged for two weeks and unpaid utility bills scattered about. Or you can go to the other extreme of obsessive tidiness. What are the ways that you ignore or are obsessed with your personal environment? List two here.

_____

_____

4 **Work space**: We spend at least one-third of our lives working, so it's really important to look at this area. Failure to manage here can take the form of phone calls not being returned, emails mounting up in your inbox, the state of your desk, being late for appointments, bringing personal problems to the office, gossip, the inability to say 'no' to additional tasks (meaning too much work), or avoiding any more responsibility. What are the signs at work which mean that you are not operating well or are stressed out? List two examples.

_____

_____

5 **Free time**: This is about stuff you like doing that's not work-related. Do you like walking, music, dancing, reading, travel, for example? List two examples of what you *stop* doing when you're 'losing the plot'.

_____

_____

6 **Social time**: Spending time with friends and colleagues is crucial to a balanced life. What are the signs when you're 'not yourself'? For example, do you isolate yourself from the world, spend too much time on Facebook, surf the dating sites or refuse to answer calls? When you're with friends, are you distracted, moody, needy or controlling? List two examples.

---

7 **Family life**: Like work, here is another area that seems to have the ability to screw us up pretty quickly if we don't watch it. List two examples of how your behaviour changes when you are disconnected from your family; for example do you have a tendency to sulk, be impatient, childish or intolerant as a way to justify what happens in your family unit?

---

8 **Finances**: How are you handling your financial responsibilities? Are you overdrawn, in debt or a real penny-pincher? List two signs of behaviour when you have money problems.

---

9 **'Me' time**: Living on self-will can make us neglect this important aspect of quiet time. Whether it's just having some quiet reading time or daydreaming, or something as organised as yoga, meditation or prayer – recharging our batteries is necessary to a truly fulfilled life. List two examples of what you neglect to do when you are too busy, not in the mood, or feeling 'burnt out'.

---

10 **Other red flags**: When our lives become unmanageable or we feel stressed or just generally discontented, we might overeat, drink too much, continually chew gum, bite our nails, self-harm, watch too much television or neglect our personal appearance. List at least three red flags that you wave when things aren't going well.

_____

_____

_____

• RECORDING YOUR WARNING SIGNS • OVER 21 DAYS

From the 20 or more warning signs that you've listed, choose the top 5 indicators of when you feel restless, irritable and discontented. Choose the ones that have bothered you for a long time, and that you can quickly pick up on when you're doing them. For example, if I spend my weekends in bed, it's a clear indicator that I need to face some instincts that are threatened and take action. When others bite their fingernails, it might be a sign they are anxious and fearful.

_____

MY TOP FIVE WARNING SIGNS

1 _____

2 _____

3 _____

4 _____

5 _____

For just 21 days, try being aware of when this objectionable behaviour pops up. Then write down what was going on when it happened and which instinct was being threatened. We'll use this information later on in Step 6, so that we can quickly do something about it.

• OPENING SOON: THE NEW ME LTD • FLAGSHIP STORE!

Remember, like the businessperson, you'll never know the value of your mind until you remove the shoddy goods from it. If the businessperson is selling substandard products they may never know how successful their business could be. But once they do a proper stocktake and fill their shelves with stuff that people want, it's a whole new ball game of success. The same is true of you.

I'll leave you with a magnificent piece of writing to help you contemplate what you have just read and give you a reason to continue.

• THE PRAYER OF ST FRANCIS •

Although recognised as one of the most beloved saints, Saint Francis was quite the libertine before undertaking a total transformation of character, conduct and consciousness. His words have an almost universal appeal, and they definitely coincide with what we're trying to do here.

My husband Bryan swears by the practicality of this passage. You can ponder over it before going into a difficult situation – such as a meeting or job interview. If you're in a state of self-centred fear, it can change your position in a few moments from a negative viewpoint to a positive one. So instead of trying to get something out of a situation (and possibly being controlled by fear or self-centredness), decide to try to contribute a healthy solution, and have the peace of mind that comes with humility, acceptance and tolerance.

You can address this to whoever or whatever you choose to be your higher power.

Make me an instrument of your peace.

Where there is hatred, let me sow love;

Where there is injury, pardon;

Where there is doubt, faith;

Where there is despair, hope;

Where there is darkness, light;

Where there is sadness, joy.

Grant that I may not so much seek

To be consoled as to console,

To be understood as to understand,

To be loved, as to love;

For it is in giving that we receive;

It is in pardoning that we are pardoned;

It is in dying to self that we are born to eternal life.

In other words, when you let go of self (your ego) and start working on removing your shortcomings, you're on the path to enjoying an abundant life.

STEP IN BRIEF

- A shortcoming is an attribute that we're short on.

- You will never be fulfilled if you continue to be controlled by your instincts.

- Discovering and removing what is objectionable to you is a continuous process which then allows something better to come into your life.

Step Five

STRAIGHTENING OUT THE PAST

• • •

**It is the highest form of self-respect to admit
our errors and mistakes and make amends for
them. To make a mistake is only an error in
judgment, but to adhere to it when it is
discovered shows infirmity of character.**

Dale Turner, author

We can't move forward until we correct the past. Making
amends is nothing more than correcting the mistakes we've
made in our life. They're not apologies – they are making a
wrong right.

• • •

• TAKING IT TO THE STREETS •

In the popular American sitcom *My Name is Earl* the main
character is a likeable small-time criminal and general rogue
who suddenly has a life revelation when it dawns on him that
bad things are happening to him because he does bad things,
and that if he does good, then he'll get good things back. He
sets about making a list of all his bad deeds and trying to put
them right. Earl calls his process of listing and making amends
'karma', but I bet one of the writers or producers is very familiar with a 12 Step programme! Call it what you like, but this
exact process is a crucial exercise in the journey towards meaningful success and happiness.

This step is about clearing away the wreckage from your personal relationships and committing to improve on those
relationships as you go forward. Why is this necessary? So far
you've made the decision in Step 2 to hand your self-will over
to some sort of power greater than you. However, if your mind
is filled with niggling memories of your behaviour, both to
yourself and others in the past, that power will not be able to
help you in the present, which is where you actually live. Your
mind is stuck in your past, rehashing and reinterpreting those
events, filling you with fear, guilt, remorse or resentment. With

all that baggage, you can't live well in the present. It's about as effective as trying to walk down a busy street whilst craning your head to see what's behind you.

So we need to look backward at your personal relationships and clear out this mixed bag of rotten goods once and for all by making amends to the people, places or things we have harmed.

Most people would rather keep their dirty laundry to themselves, thinking: '*If I admit that I was wrong, people may spot a weakness and take advantage of me*' or '*She's just as bad as me, so why the hell should I apologise?*' There's that ego again in a different costume, this time masquerading as pride and hiding behind self-justification.

Naturally, this is going to be a daunting idea, because for the first time in this programme you have to actually do something that involves someone else. This may put your mind at ease: the two Steps that people generally wince at in this programme are Step 3 and this Step. Sadly most people baulk at them, stay stuck in their negative behaviours and deny themselves the chance to build upon their character. You, on the other hand, have started to take these Steps, and whether you know it or not, you are beginning to change, and an 'unsuspected inner resource' (as they say in AA) is beginning to flow into you. That resource will be there to support you as you take this Step.

You could be thinking this might be a pointless exercise – you know, opening up old wounds, some of them very deep, many of them forgotten – why do it? I thought the same myself, and I only realised the benefit of this Step once I had done it. More about that later.

• SO HERE'S HOW YOU DO IT •

1 You make a list of the people that you've harmed.
2 You become willing to make amends to them.
3 You make direct amends to them wherever possible except
   when to do so would injure them or others.

Before we get into the details it may be useful to look at what we
mean by 'harms'. What kind of harms do people do to each
other? Bill Wilson in *The Twelve Steps and the Twelve Traditions*
describes a harm as the result of *'instincts in collision which cause
physical, mental, emotional or spiritual damage to people'* (p. 80).
When we have an attitude that's fearful, selfish, dishonest or
inconsiderate, we step on other people's toes and threaten their
basic instincts. We disturb them and possibly cause them to
retaliate.

Harmful behaviours might include lying, cheating or stealing,
even if it is only company time surfing the Web when we should
be working, or letting a friend down with a lame or untrue
excuse. It might be spendthrift or miserly behaviour, both of
which affect the comfort of others in the end. Or it might be
about our sexual conduct that may be out of kilter, which gen-
erates deep wounds, anger, suspicion and misery.

The most important amend we need to make is to ourselves. When
you've been running on misdirected instincts for most of your
life, either as a control freak or a perceived 'doormat' tending to
everyone else's needs, you've probably neglected yourself and it
makes it a lot easier to make amends to others if we first practise on ourselves.

There are in fact two types of amends to review and make:

1 **Face-to-face amends** from your inventory lists, for example, being intolerant of your mother, padding your expense account or an extramarital affair.

2 **Financial amends**: Some of you may owe money; this can range from loans from our friends and family to large amounts on credit cards or bank loans.

Both types need your attention.

• FACE-TO-FACE AMENDS •

We'll start with these personal amends. Get hold of your inventory sheets once more, and starting with your Resentment list – go immediately to column 4. Now look again at the 'exact nature' of the wrong, in other words see your part in the problem and then you can perhaps understand why the person you resent may have retaliated – column 2. If that's the case it was you who started the ball rolling, and therefore it's you who owes the amend and not the other way round. So put this person or place down on your amends list. If your ego is still opening its big mouth, let's look again at what Bill Wilson says in *Twelve Steps and Twelve Traditions*:

> The moment we ponder a twisted or broken relationship with another person, our emotions go on the defensive. To escape looking at the wrongs we have done another, we resentfully focus on the wrong he has done us. This is especially true if he has, in fact, behaved badly at all. Triumphantly we seize on his misbehaviour as the perfect excuse for minimising or forgetting our own (p. 78).

The same goes for your Fears list. Look at column 4 – what action or emotion in you has caused you to feel this fear? Go back to columns 1 and 2 and put on your amends list anyone that you need to face to get over this fear.

Your Sex and Harms to Others inventory is next. Look at column 1 and put those names down on your amends list also.

While you're at it, think of anyone or anything else that you have hurt or harmed and put those down on your amends list – be sure to follow the inventory process through with these late additions too.

I've taken an example from each inventory sheet given in Step 3, and completed the form opposite to help give you an idea of how to do this.

SO YOU'VE MADE YOUR LIST, WHAT NEXT?

The most important thing now is that you become genuinely willing to make the amend. Once again, that old chestnut willingness is the key to a successful Step 5. Now there is no way that you will be able to make amends to all of the people on your list, and this could be for a variety of reasons:

- You've lost contact with the person.
- They're no longer alive.
- You may lose your job.
- You could injure yourself or someone else even more.
- You could be prosecuted.

WHO DO WE START WITH?

A simple and effective way to begin this essential process is to make a chart with the headings:

NOW   LATER   MAYBE   NEVER

Review of Amends

| | COLUMN 1 | COLUMN 2 | COLUMN 3 — Affects my... (Which part of self caused the harm?) | | | | | | | | | COLUMN 4 — What is the exact nature of my wrongs, faults, mistakes, defects, shortcomings? | | | |
| | Who did I harm? | What did I do? | Social instinct | | Security instinct | | Sex instinct | | Ambitions | | | | | | |
			Self-esteem	Relationships	Material	Emotional	Acceptable sex relations	Hidden sex relations	Social	Security	Sexual	Selfish	Dishonest	Self-Seeking/Frightened	Inconsiderate
1	My company	Because I think I'm paid poorly. I'm a 'jobs-worth', a moaner and a saboteur	✓	✓	✓	✓			✓	✓		✓	✓	✓	✓
2	Me	I've done nothing to increase my chances of meeting someone and have	✓	✓		✓	✓		✓	✓	✓	✓	✓	✓	✓
3	My work colleague's wife	I had sex with her husband	✓	✓		✓	✓		✓		✓	✓	✓	✓	✓

NOW: In this list include people whom you see often and who need an amend. These can be close friends and family, any work colleagues, your supervisor or your neighbour.

LATER: Again, you know you have harmed this person or organisation, but they are more difficult to reach. For example, I contacted an old boss of mine four years after I had left the company to apologise for my unprofessional behaviour during my notice period. I lived in a different city and even though the issue occurred in the past, when I eventually got the opportunity I contacted her. I know of people who try to make their amends via email. This is OK – but only if you caused the harm via email! If you really can't meet a person face to face, then a phone call will do if all else fails.

MAYBE: This is often the biggest lump to swallow. On your list here is perhaps a person who has retaliated. These will be the names of people from your Resentment list, those who have harmed you, but now you can understand from your inventory analysis that you started the problem. This is why these types of amends are number three on your timeline. It's best if you get used to practising the process and seeing the results before you 'lead with the chin' as you don't want to put your size 43s in and fall at the first hurdle. Experiences among many people who have made this type of amend show that even our most bitter rivals will often meet us halfway.

NEVER: On this list will be various people with whom you may never be able to clear up the past – but it doesn't absolve you from being *willing* to do so.

- For example, those who are no longer alive. Here a 'living' amend is suggested. So, if you have hurt your father, and he is no longer alive, you could make a living amend by being more helpful and kind to your mother, or supporting one of his favourite causes, or just living the way you think he would want his son or daughter to live. Some people I know have written a letter to the person. Those who are really serious about making the amend and freeing themselves totally even write a reply to their letter. Try it, it may not be as bizarre as you think!

• The other amend on your Never list is if you were to make the amend it could cause injury, either to yourself or another. For example, number 3 on our Harms list (p. 127): we wouldn't go to the wife and apologise; it would potentially cause great damage and totally destroy the marriage. Do you really want to be responsible for causing more chaos? Or if you have been padding your expense account, it may not be prudent to admit this to your boss (unless he asked you first!). Stopping it would be a more effective way of moving forward and helping your company prosper.

Here's a personal example: I wanted to write to my old long-term boyfriend. He lived hundreds of miles away so I thought it would be a good idea to set down on paper the things I had done wrong in our relationship. Now this man was number 1, 2 and 3 on my Resentment list – he had left me for someone else. My letter made some weak mumblings about how I couldn't blame him for leaving me, etc., but then I went on to explain my own great achievements to him, how I was doing brilliantly and my life was full. I felt really good about this amend. Thankfully I showed this letter to my guide before I posted it; she observed:

> 'What if he is married now? He and his wife won't want a blast from the past coming back into his life; they may even have children, and you could cause more damage.'

'What is your real motive behind this amend? This letter just looks like a thinly disguised revenge letter, showing him how well you are doing without him.'

She was right on both counts and I didn't send the letter. So at this point I had to accept that it would be a living amend, and if our paths cross in the future I would be willing to put the matter right.

• FINANCIAL AMENDS •

Here is your chance to be free from the terror of looking at those brown envelopes that come in the post. If you owe money, then the people or institutions you owe it to should be put on your Review of Harms list. Sorting your finances out is a great step to removing fear and resentment. Once again, the key here is willingness.

If you are overwhelmed by your debt many agencies exist to assist you. My husband Bryan went to one of these, cut up his credit cards in front of them, contacted his creditors, negotiated an interest 'amnesty', devised a monthly payment plan, and within three years he was free of a £20,000 debt.

Don't be afraid to contact your creditors. It may surprise you that, as long as you show some integrity, willingness and discipline, more often than not they will take what's on offer.

Even if you don't owe a pile of money, get that £10 paid back to your friend you borrowed it from a year ago. If there is one thing I have learned in my personal and business life it is that nobody forgets when they lend you money, and it doesn't matter how small the amount is. Clear away your debt, £1 at a time, and become financially independent again. This will give you:

- a healthy talent for sacrificing what you want as opposed to what you need;
- a new disciplined attitude, which is another part of this programmed of being fulfilled;
- a huge boost to your self-esteem.

DEBT BUSTER

Complete this if you think you need to. There's no need for instructions – there usually never is when it comes to money!

Debt amount	To whom owed	Action needed	Time frame

• REACTION, REACTION, REACTION •

Now how about the response you're likely to receive? Well, first of all, let's get this clear: this is not about the other person's reaction, it is about you clearing your side of the street. *You have no control over their responses; all you are responsible for is setting right your wrongs.* What's the possibility that you'll be snubbed or thrown out of an office or home? Practically non-existent.

In my personal experience, along with listening to hundreds of success stories about people making amends, the upshot is that feuds of many years just melt away. If you want proof of this just watch an episode of *My Name is Earl* – the reactions he gets are about what you can expect also. There are equally a number of people who have made an amend and the person they are making it to can't even remember the incident. This surprises many, in fact some even pick up a new resentment about the fact that they have been smouldering over this issue for years and the other person hasn't given it a second thought! The overwhelming evidence of the millions of people who have embarked on this programme of action is that there is usually a sense of relief on all sides.

• A LIFETIME STEP •

This process of straightening out the past won't be over and done with by next Thursday. This challenging step requires patience, good timing and a clear head, but more than anything else it needs you to make a start. If you put off this step, you'll only invite pride and procrastination to convince you that making amends doesn't apply to you. Here are a few tips about taking this step forward:

1 **An apology with an excuse is not an apology, it is a justification.** You must rid your mind of any justifications for why you behaved the way you did. Keep your mind in the fourth column of your inventory. If you don't, this step will backfire and the person you're making amends to will wipe the floor with you. Believe me.

2 **Realise that it's OK to admit you're not perfect.** My husband tells of a funny encounter he had in a local DIY store. He was pushing a trolley down an aisle and not watching where he was going, and tapped his trolley into that of an elderly couple. Being a polite American, he quickly said 'Excuse me', and the older man said with a

wag of his finger and a wink of his eye: 'Don't apologise, it's a sign of weakness.' *With this step, you'll discover that it's the stronger person who can admit they're at fault.*

3 **Ask for help.** Just 'how' you make the amend is as important as making it. It will help if you reflect a little around the personalities involved. It may be useful to explain the situation to your guide. Since they're not emotionally involved, they'll help you to see it clearly, and to go into the situation without being hot-headed.

4 **Be willing and available.** Often you won't need to make a special visit to someone, especially those on your Now list, as you'll probably be bumping into them sometime soon. So bide your time: it may just be in conversation around the coffee machine, or during your appraisal with your boss, or while you're having Sunday lunch with your parents, or down at the local pub with your friends.

5 **Take it easy and ask for help from your higher power.** Too often we get wound up about the thought of doing something, gird our loins and charge into a situation using force (instead of power). Go with the flow.

6 **Don't delay because of fear.** You've come so far and discovered so much about yourself and your world. Don't you think it's about time you faced the consequences of your past life, thought about those you have damaged and moved on? Try to imagine just how liberating that will feel.

7 **Enjoy the domino principle.** There's a reason we put the names into columns of Now, Later, Maybe, Never. When you take care of the Nows, the Laters will move into their position. It will get easier facing the people that you've avoided, just as it has for the millions of people across the world who have done this before.

• WHAT DO I SAY? •

HOW TO APOLOGISE: A SIX-POINT PLAN

For many of you, the thought of this Step will be extremely tough, and some of you may not have apologised properly for years.

So here's a simple *'How to'* guide:

1 **Write your apology down.** Sometimes this helps – a letter format works well. Read and rehearse it if you need to.

2 **Name the wrong.** For example:
   - 'I'm sorry that I haven't spent time with you and Mum, I've been totally inconsiderate.'
   - 'I'm sorry that I didn't pay you back the £100 sooner, it was wrong of me.'
   - 'I'm sorry that I took your customer, I hope it didn't leave a gaping hole in your sales figures.'

3 **Make the amend.** Think about why you caused the harm (you may have been one of the following: *selfish, self-centred, dishonest, inconsiderate or afraid*) and let the person know. Also tell them how you will avoid making that mistake in the future, for example:
   - 'I ignored your wedding invitation because I thought I was too busy. That was inconsiderate of me, and I'm sorry. *Is there any way I can make amends?*'
   - 'I've not been performing here (at work) lately. I've been self-centred and resentful about Julie getting the promotion and I was wrong. *Starting tomorrow I'm going to change my attitude.*'
   - 'Do you remember when your car was scratched last

year? I did that because I was resentful towards you. I'm sorry and I want to clear it up. *How much did the repair job cost?*'

● 'I know that I've been suspicious and starting rows for some time now. I was jealous and afraid that you were losing interest in me, I was wrong. *How can I make it up to you?*'

4 **Be understanding.** If the apology is not accepted, thank them for listening to you and leave the door open. Whatever happens don't get involved in retaliatory arguments. Keep it simple. Make your amend and move on.

5 **Be patient.** Just because someone accepts your apology doesn't mean that they have forgiven you. It takes time to trust again and, just like you, other people have the right to feel the pain of having their basic instincts threatened.

6 **Don't tell me, show me.** Now is your opportunity to stick to your word and show that this isn't an empty gesture. The next two steps of this programme are dedicated to showing you how to do just that.

● SEEING THE RESULTS: THE PROMISES ●

Step 5 finishes off the action tasks in this programme. Don't rest on your laurels just yet though and be prepared for a continuous process of repairing and improving relationships.

You've come a long way in starting to remove your major issues of resentment, fears, guilt and harms done to others – the very things that have been blocking you from achieving lasting fulfilment. So where are the rewards of this bone-crushing ego blaster of a programme?

Trust me, if you've done what is suggested to the best of your ability, and if you've made an honest effort to practice these age-old principles for living, then you're probably already receiving 'the promises'. These often-read words have become true for millions of people, and they certainly came true for me.

> If we are painstaking about this phase of our development, we will be amazed before we are halfway through:
>
> We are going to know a new freedom and a new happiness.
>
> We will not regret the past nor wish to shut the door on it.
>
> We will comprehend the word serenity and we will know peace.
>
> No matter how far down the scale we have gone, we will see how our experience can benefit others.
>
> That feeling of uselessness and self-pity will slip away.
>
> Our whole attitude and outlook upon life will change.
>
> Fear of people and of economic insecurity will leave us.
>
> We will intuitively know how to handle situations that used to baffle us.
>
> Bill Wilson, *Big Book of Alcoholics Anonymous,*. (p. 84)

Bill Wilson concludes that we will suddenly realise that our new-found power is doing for us what we could not do for ourselves.

What strikes me now, and maybe you'll agree, is that the feelings these 'promises' gave me were what I had been chasing all my life – but I had no idea how to get there. I tried booze, achievement, cunning, manipulation – and none of it worked.

You see, my problem was a lack of knowledge about myself and other people. I really had no idea about what made us all tick. I do now. And because I do, I refuse to pay the price of ignorance and I choose to become fully accountable for all that happens in my life. By following this programme I tapped into the 'unsuspected inner resource' – pure power. Before finding this way to live I had experienced life through my feelings and senses – force, in other words.

This self-awareness and new-found knowledge gave me the courage to decide to start my business from scratch and then take it to a successful exit, it made me unselfish enough to embark on a loving relationship, gave me the patience to be a decent mother, the honesty to be a good friend and the humility not to take credit for these achievements. There is no way I could have done any of this without this programme.

And I'm not special: I'm only one among millions for whom this has worked, so you have every right to believe it will work for you.

The next two Steps are dedicated to helping us keep these promises in our lives.

STEP IN BRIEF

- Making amends is the final task in clearing up the past.

- If you shy away from this Step you will always be blocked from being fulfilled.

- As long as you have a willingness to make an amend, the situation will present itself at the proper time.

- If you do this, the result will be a new freedom and a new happiness that comes from this personality change.

Step Six

STAYING THE COURSE – A BETTER WAY TO LIVE EVERY DAY

• • •

Look to this day,
For it is life,
The very life of life.
In its brief course lie all
The realities and verities of existence,
The bliss of growth,
The splendour of action,
The glory of power –

For yesterday is but a dream
And tomorrow is only a vision,
But today, well lived,
Makes every yesterday a dream of happiness,
And every tomorrow a vision of hope.
Look well therefore to this day.

Sanskrit proverb

So where are we at this stage? If you've been thorough and open-minded so far, then you've made tremendous progress in this 'solution-oriented, problem-solving process'. And I imagine you're starting to see the results of your efforts. Rest assured, *you are changing* – even though you may be the last one to see it.

The quality of your life is now down to you. And as the Sanskrit proverb says, this is your time and all you have is this day. What you think and do during these 24 hours will be the key to enjoying tomorrow. This step will show you how to keep your newly acquired rose-tinted glasses rosy – even when they get steamed up.

• • •

Before you can say I can't, say. . . I'll try.

Anonymous

• QUICK! FIX ME UP WITH THE • £9.99 SPECIAL

Consider where you are at this point: you may now be sensing a new freedom from those old fears and resentments, perhaps you're even excited about what the future holds. Possibly you're just feeling more at ease with the world than you did before you started reading this book. Whether you know it or not, what you've just cracked is a code for living a life that befits a human being of courage and integrity, and yes, that does include you!

Gone are the days when you needed to 'white knuckle' your way through each 24 hours. If you've completed the Steps so far, just look how far you've come: You've courageously faced your past and learned that your ego is something to befriend. You know that all of your problems and subsequent feelings are the result of out-of-kilter basic instincts, equally now you have a technique to let these defects go. This is your opportunity to be free from yourself once and for all. Self-knowledge rather than self-doubt is soon to become your guiding force.

A friend of mine tells it like this:

> What this programme has given me is a bit of freedom from the constant struggle in my mind of trying to control my reactions to the world around me. For instance, recently I was training a group of people and one of them pointed out something that I'd forgotten to say. Normally my mind would snap on that as a challenge to my 'prestige', and I'd have to pounce on that person. I didn't see it at the time, but then I'd start a tennis match of resentments and retaliations spread out over days or weeks.
>
> Knowing this weakness in myself, I would then try to control my tongue, but there would always be the tug of war in my mind about whether I should follow my instincts – which told me to snap at them – or to just let it pass.
>
> Now that I've been through these Steps and become acquainted with my instincts, my ego, my defects, and what my part is in all this, today I can let what people say pass through me and I don't have to react, nor do I have the turmoil of trying to decide whether I need to react. And when I do need to address something, I just

**say my bit in a calm voice and it's no longer a fight
between me and the world.**

This programme delivers on its promises. If you trust the process
it will continue to bring you happiness and personal fulfilment, it
will show you how to handle any and every situation and it will
give you constant guidance about how to live. Personally I think
we're all very lucky to have discovered this toolkit for life.

The great thing is, there's plenty more to learn. So what's next?

• TIME TAKES TIME •

What I've learned is that *there are no long-lasting quick fixes;
staying fulfilled requires a lifetime of work and effort.* Trust me,
I've been at it for 18 years and I still have to lift my pick and
shovel every day to chip away at life. I know you may be
thinking that you've just gone through the personal wringer,
and the thought of more of the same may be as appealing as
swimming off the Scottish coast on Christmas Day, but frankly,
nothing short of continuous action will keep you here and get
you there (or get you to where you want to be).

Take a look at where you are in this programme. In Steps 1 and
2 you expressed the problem and the solution; this didn't
require any action, you just needed to recognise your problem
(powerlessness) and make a decision to find the solution
(power). You didn't really grow personally here, because you
were still blocked by the baggage from your past (resentments
and harms) and the bogeymen of the future (your fears). Then,
in Steps 3–5, you took some action and worked to remove what
had been blocking you from finding this power. This act of
unblocking is where your personality change began happening.

One other thing that this unblocking has done, and you may not have noticed, is that you're beginning to experience the world differently. You see, along with your five senses that you use to experience the world, you're now developing a sixth sense – a positive, creative inflow that some people call *intuition*. This has always been there in you just as it was in me; it's just that I had no idea how to access it and perhaps this is the same with you.

But let me hammer this home: this way of living requires practice and a continual revisiting of Steps 1–5 each day. Compare it to an endless, wonderful red carpet that is being rolled out in front of you – but behind you, two guys are rolling up that red carpet. So we have to keep walking.

> **Remember: change – if you really want it – is a process, not an event.**

• STAYING CENTRED WITH A • DAILY MOT

WHY DO WE NEED TO DO THIS?

This new way of living and thinking can disappear subtly if we don't carry on submerging our ego. The ego is always there, and it will be with us for the rest of our days. And if we let it, it's easy to return to our old way of dealing with uncomfortable feelings, that is, dealing with them from the 'outside in' – you know, the old routine of: 'They did that to me', 'He took this from me', 'She hurt me', 'I can't do that, I'll fail', your old version of 'the truth'. Today you've been given the tools to look at yourself accurately – from the inside out, and live in a victim-free way. But as an old-timer in this programme has said: '*It's always going to be like speaking a second language; we'll always speak it with an accent.'*

Personally, it took me around eight months to get to this stage in the programme, and I wanted to keep this new-found power. You see, I was about to leave Japan and backpack through Asia and the promises that I spoke of in the previous chapter were slowly beginning to happen to me – note that I said 'beginning'. I was still broke and doing many things my way, but I'd come a long way in self-knowledge and had taken the suggested actions, which had begun to give me a sense of real inner power and I wanted to keep it. I suppose you do too. To be honest with you, I was unsure what appalled me more: not keeping this feeling I'd discovered or slipping back into my old ways. I was reminded over and over again that constant working of these Steps was the only way to do both. So here's what was suggested to me that I do every day as I went off on my travels, to keep me motivated, balanced and confident, and this is what I'm passing on to you.

INTRODUCING: THE SPOT CHECK INVENTORY

REVISIT YOUR WARNING SIGNS: It's crucial to be aware of how your thinking and feelings are manifesting themselves throughout your day. And our feelings are the easiest indicators for us to spot. Go back to your list of the top five crazy behaviours you recorded in Step 4 and reinforce them in your mind.

These behaviours are like indicator lights on your dashboard (i.e. brake warning lights that tell you to get your car checked immediately). If you ignore one of these indicators on your dashboard and say to yourself, 'I'm too busy to get my brakes checked', the problem is just going to get worse, and more expensive to repair.

It's the same with your behaviour. Just as we have signs to show us when physical health is affected such as a cough or fever, we also have indicators when our spiritual health is affected such as *fear, guilt, resentment or remorse*. These indicators may be disguised as other feelings (which is why I've included an Emotions chart), but if you scratch the surface of most painful feelings the root cause is generally one of these.

Always ask:

- Am I being selfish?
- Am I being inconsiderate?
- Am I being dishonest?
- Am I being fearful?
- Am I being self-seeking?

EMOTIONS CHART

Don't you just hate lists? Well, take a good look at the one on the following page, as it may just save you from an emotional binge one day. It covers almost anything you could be feeling in any 24 hours – along with its antidote. I'm calling it an antidote, because a lot of the stuff we feel is like a virus in our minds, and when we have a harmful virus we generally take prompt action, don't we? Otherwise we deteriorate physically very quickly.

It's the same with our emotions, feelings and subsequent actions, we need to spot the problem and act to remove it – the quicker the better. So, the next time you are feeling *restless, irritable and discontented* about something and can't quite put your finger on it, take a look through this chart – you'll see your issue somewhere in this list.

Personality characteristics of self-will	Personality characteristics of good-will
Selfishness and self-seeking	Interest in others
Dishonesty	Honesty
Fear	Courage
Lack of consideration	Consideration
Pride	Humility
Greed	Giving or sharing
Lust	Doing for others
Anger	Calmness
Envy	Gratitude
Procrastination	Taking action
Gluttony	Moderation
Impatience	Patience
Intolerance	Tolerance
Resentment	Forgiveness
Hate	Love – concern for others
Harmful acts	Good deeds
Self-pity	Self-forgiveness
Self-justification	Humility
Self-importance	Modesty
Self-condemnation	Self-forgiveness
Suspicion	Trust
Doubt	Faith

Adapted from McQuany, J. 'Daily Inventory' from *Carry This Message* (p. 135)
(Reprinted with kind permission of the Kelly Foundation.)

SO WHAT DO WE DO NOW?

Well, *pain is unavoidable, but misery is optional,* and the brilliant thing is we don't have to wallow in this bog for a long time. So the next time you have resentment, a fear or a guilty feeling, trace the emotion through: mentally take yourself through the inventory process (through all four columns). Then look at what basic instinct has been harmed and then which character defect has surfaced.

HOW TO DO THE SPOT-CHECK INVENTORY

- Spot the emotion (from the Emotions chart).
- Identify the basic instinct that was threatened (i.e. all the different aspects of social, security or sex instincts).
- Claim your part (ask yourself if you were selfish, inconsiderate, self-seeking, dishonest, fearful).
- Admit to yourself that you need help to have it removed.
- Let it go.
- Get feedback from your guide if you need it.

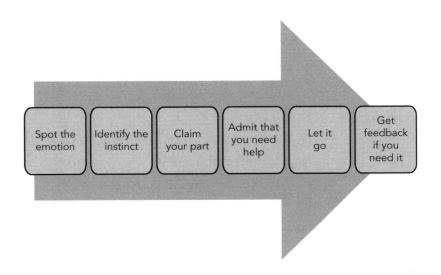

Spot the emotion | Identify the instinct | Claim your part | Admit that you need help | Let it go | Get feedback if you need it

YOU'RE THE ONLY PROBLEM

... AND YOU'RE THE ONLY SOLUTION:

To date, you, I and most of the world have been intoxicated with 'blame culture', high on finger-pointing. This keeps us stuck, preventing us from truly moving forward and being who we were always intended to be. Now you've got a programme to live by and your goals can be realised more quickly. Not only that, you've also got a tried and tested method of taking full responsibility for your life, and this might as well be your ultimate goal because everything that you do will flow from this little nugget: you are the only solution. In any event, what's the alternative? Your ego, waiting patiently like a crouching tiger looking for its bait, desperate to take you hostage again.

So this step is the maintenance step. It requires you to continue the process every day, admit when your thinking or actions have been off beam, and apologise, without delay, when you are wrong. What you do today will impact on tomorrow so it doesn't take a brain surgeon to see that if you want a successful and fulfilling future you need to curtail – or at least learn from – your emotional excesses today. This is why continuing to take a personal inventory on a daily basis is so vital to your sustained contentment.

Real Life Stories

66 The first step in making progress is to admit our mistakes. To back this up, here are examples of both my personal experiences and from other people who are following this programme and continuing to take a spot check inventory.

● I was speaking at a large conference recently and as an ex-comedienne I began the talk with a joke that was aimed at the guy who organised the event. I realised immediately I'd said it how inappropriate it was. So after my 45-minute keynote I went straight to him and apologised and explained that I was wrong to take out my nervousness at someone else's expense. **Result:** No prolonged guilty feeling, and no resentment towards me.

- After starting this programme years ago my husband had a real problem in keeping his temper on the road. He found that he had to put a Post-it note on his steering wheel that said 'Let it go.' This was a helpful way of reminding him that he had no control over other drivers and the only thing to do was to let go of his feelings of anger, feelings he could trace back to his security instincts (being stepped on by other drivers), and that he realised he could further trace back to his own lack of consideration for other drivers. **Results:** Less stress on the road and arriving at his appointments in a better mood.

- Tony is a reasonably good swimmer and was disappointed to find that the only lane open in the swimming pool was one where elderly ladies were taking a leisurely swim. He wanted to take some vigorous exercise, so unmindful of their welfare he barged past them doing front crawl. After four or five lengths he sensed that this wasn't appropriate. He apologised to them all for his behaviour and joined in the leisurely swim with them. **Result:** No remorse, no selfishness, a show of tolerance and a nice chat!

- I was travelling back from London to Leeds by train on a Saturday afternoon. I was late and ravenous, so just before getting on the train I bought a bag of chips and sat in the first-class carriage. Sitting in the carriage across from me were a couple who were obviously disturbed by the smell of the chips. They glared at me and muttered to each other how distasteful eating chips in a first-class carriage was. I felt so uncomfortable that I couldn't eat the chips, so I wrapped them up well and put them in the bin. The couple then stood up with their bags full of designer purchases and announced to each other that they were moving carriages because of the offending smell. Now how did I feel? For a moment, angry: they had humiliated me in front of other people. Then I tried to deal with it differently. You know, maybe they had a point: travelling first class is very expensive and perhaps this was an annual treat for them and the chips had spoiled it. Also, it was pretty inconsiderate of me not to think of the other travellers on the train. **Result**: No feelings of resentment. I let it go, it took me about 30 minutes to see my part, but I let it go – and ate some odourless grapes instead!

● During my morning run I use the time and personal space to think. Most days, my thoughts are positive and creative and I'm grateful for the abundance in my life. Occasionally, my thoughts are black, miserable and even vengeful. As I'm trotting along (I'm not a very fast runner!), I could be thinking these dark thoughts for five or ten minutes, enjoying the rush of the dull pain that they give me. When I catch myself with these thoughts I really do try hard to remove them by thinking of something more positive – my children, my husband Bryan (that's if the dark thoughts aren't about him!), the sky, the trees or whatever. It requires effort though. **Result**: I know if I don't change my thoughts the day ahead will be more difficult than it needs to be, and Deirdre is the one in charge of Deirdre's day.

- Simon, a friend of mine, was annoyed because an Audi owner (obviously a friend of his neighbour's) always parks in his spot outside his house every weekend, forcing Simon to park up the road. He was about to put a note under the car's windscreen wipers. I pointed out to him that this would be inconsiderate as the road is public property, and the neighbour's friend has a right to park where he wants. I also let him know he could expect some sort of retaliation if he put a note on the car demanding it be moved. Like most of us, he needs a dispute with his neighbours like a hole in the head. A good rule of thumb in times of disagreement or difficulty is to ask yourself, '*Would I rather be right or happy*?' Now that's a good **Result**! " "

CONCLUSION

Challenge yourself to do this – see it as a personal project. Life does become exciting because, in a bizarre way, you are actually more in control. How does that work? From this self-knowledge comes power, and you'll find, just as I did, that with continued effort you'll come to see the benefit of changing your thinking and feelings. When you do this your actions change automatically as the personality characteristics of 'good-will' flow into you and slowly become a way of life.

The benefit of that is plain to see – you are in much less danger of excitement, fear or worry. Because of your positive outlook, people will come into your life, you'll find that they want to be around you, you will attract much more of what you want – those promises outlined in the last Step will come to you and stay with you and you'll have a new-found self-confidence that's not based on arrogance and fear, but on humility. Surprisingly, you'll discover that it is humility which shows us that we are good enough, and not our relentless chase for success. Doesn't this sound too good to be true?

Life seems to get a bit easier and even fun. You can get on with what you need to do in a day rather than wasting valuable time and energy thinking about things that you can't control – generally other people, places and things.

• STAYING SERENE THROUGH • SELF-REFLECTION

Rise and shine! The alarm clock rings, we jump out of bed and begin the ritual of another day. Just like robots – we've done it so many times we don't even have to think about what we're doing. We grit our teeth through the broken shoelace, the spilt coffee or the forgotten homework, and we're on the road to another frustrating day, effectively saying in the words of cartoonist Charles Schulz: 'I love mankind; it's people I can't stand.'

There is an easier way to live than racing through the day blurting out 'Sorry!' when we've done something wrong or feel the sting of our negative thoughts – it's called *self-reflection*. By practising this, it's as if we are inflating the tyres on our car: we can go over the bumps in the road with ease. If we don't practise this, we're like the car with under-inflated tyres, and every bump that we hit rattles our teeth.

WHAT IS SELF-REFLECTION?

Self-reflection is taking our method of inventory one step further. Call it what you like, but ultimately this is a spiritual programme of action. Please don't confuse this with religion – the two are separate. Spirituality simply implies an open mindedness to the possibility that there is something more than the material world.

You're now at the place where you are completing what you began to do in Step 2, that is, *making a decision* to hand over your ego to your higher power as you understand it, and coming to believe you are not the centre of the universe. You're now at a place where you can do it, since you've removed the blockages from acting on that decision. Now it's time to learn the simple, powerful tool to keep what you've just found, which is trying to get a closer connection to your higher power or the universe or whatever you want to call it.

THE FOURTH DIMENSION: TAPPING INTO YOUR INNER RESOURCE

You and I live in a three-dimensional universe. Suppose there were another dimension, just as real, but outside of our usual intellectual (and highly subjective) experience. Some people call this the fourth dimension – some people call it *intuition*. Let's see if we can approach it.

THE FOURTH DIMENSION OF LIFE: Rather than basing our ideas on what we can grasp outside of us and then trying to bring it into our reality, let's look at dimensions and experience another way: from the inside out. From your physics class you'll remember that everything in the universe operates like this – subatomic particles, atoms, molecules, which make up the stuff we see and touch. If a medical researcher wants to find a cure for a disease, he goes from the level of the body right down into the components of cells to find the answers.

In the same way, you and I have levels, and in this programme we've been working from the inside out all the while. We looked at our basic instincts and ego problem, then went on to see how that problem affects our behaviour, and then we took that awareness up a level to see how we interact with other people, and to clear things up with society.

In other words, and again moving from the inside out, we have a central dimension, the 'spiritual', then we have our instincts, which include our emotions, then we move out towards our physical environment.

So if we understand that life itself starts from the inside out, then *why do we try constantly to work life from the outside in?* We

THE THREE DIMENSIONS OF LIFE: STEPS 1–7

There are three dimensions of life:
1st   Spiritual   Steps 1 and 2
2nd Mental   Steps 3 and 4
3rd   Physical and Social Steps 5 – 7

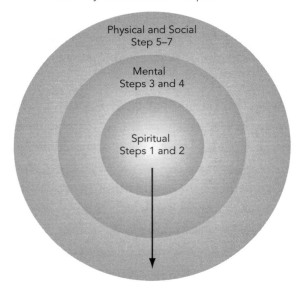

focus on the 'externals' in the hope that that will make us feel better. Have you ever heard of the phrase 'he's off beam', meaning 'he's out of kilter, out of balance'? When our central core is out of balance we try to get stuff to fill it – the 'hole in the soul' it's called. We load ourselves up with our need for approval, a bigger house, a better car, designer shoes, a new partner, drugs, sex, booze, bingo, or whatever. We'll take anything that can fill the emptiness, the void in our centre. This, as you know only too well, is merely a temporary fix.

But we're trying a different way – we're going to the inside and we're working from the inside out. You see, if we can follow these principles for living and grow spiritually and emotionally, we'll have a better relationship with our physical world and then we'll get a chance to touch the 'fourth dimension'. There are limits on three dimensions of life because there are limits on the human mind and body. The fourth dimension, the spirit, is limitless though – it's like you're tapping into a giant database of genius. Imagine that? Imagine what you can do once you get connected to this and start working from the inside out – there will be no limit to what you can do and your life will never be the same again.

How do I know this? Well, having gone from being a broken person with limited experience of most things in life to a life of remarkable success and fulfilment in a short period of time, I know the only major thing I've done is admit my powerlessness and surrender my ego. Luck had nothing to do with it, as there are plenty of other people who were more experienced in all walks of life than me. It's nothing short of miraculous. It can be for you too, as it has been for millions across the world.

DON'T INTELLECTUALISE – UTILISE

So just how do you tap into this 'inner resource', which for most of us has been lying dormant for years? Plenty of ways. The most usual are meditation, prayer, yoga or something similar. This will be easy to relate to for some, for others – well, you might just think that's not really your 'bag'.

But here's a suggestion for the militant doubters: to try meditation, prayer and guidance, just as an experiment. AA founder Bill Wilson was a militant doubter and a protégé of Thomas Edison, before drink tripped him up. Here's what he says:

> **He can address himself to whatever God he thinks there is. Or, if he thinks there is none, he can admit – just for experimental purposes – that he might be wrong. This is all-important. As soon as he is able to take this attitude, it means that he has stopped playing God himself; his mind has opened. Like any good scientist in his laboratory, our friend can assume a theory and pray to a 'higher power' that _may_ exist and _may_ be willing to help and guide him. Again he tries to behave like the scientist, an experimenter who is never supposed to give up so long as there is a vestige of any chance of success.**

> _The Language of the Heart_ (p. 241)

Give it a go, what have you got to lose? If nothing else, you're working this programme by accepting that you're not the 'be all and end all' of your world; view it as a practice lesson in humility.

• REVIEWING YOUR DAY •

1 NIGHTLY REVIEW

Depending on your lifestyle, generally the best times for review are when we go to bed and upon waking, and in that order. There is an old saying: 'The darkest hour is before the dawn', and how true that is. How often have you gone to bed worrying, fretting or angry about what happened during the day? Your senses are on overload when you are tired (that's why it is never a good idea to send an angry email or text message at night). The last thing you want to do is take those feelings into your dream state with you, and wake up with an emotional hangover.

Instead, think about the day that you've just lived while it's still fresh in your mind, and ask:

- What did you do well today and can you improve upon it tomorrow?
- Did any defects rear their ugly head?
- Were you inconsiderate, fearful, selfish, dishonest, self-seeking?
- Do you owe anyone an apology, including yourself?

So instead of stewing about what other people have done to you today, ask what you did or whether your thinking was wrong.

The day is still fresh so this is a good time to reflect on how well you performed this programme. Be rigorously honest. You know where you have come from, so evaluate your progress and measure it against where you want to be. If you are having difficulty with anything, hand your issue over and ask for guidance to be shown the right thing to do.

2 MORNING REVIEW

This is a wonderful time to connect to your higher power and it's also the most practical, as you've got a day to live ahead of you. Generally, you'll be fresh from a good night's sleep. So why not improve your whole day, by setting your alarm 15 minutes earlier and taking the time to get your mind ready to face the day?

FIRST: READ AND LISTEN: Find a quiet place, perhaps read something calming, thoughtful or spiritual, reflect on the words you read, relate them to a current event in your life. Relax and listen to what's going on in your mind. If you have any feelings of fear, anxiety or selfishness, simply surrender those. Let your mind clear. Don't force it to clear – the goal is not to be free of thoughts, but just to watch them. If a disturbing thought pops up (and it will, your ego hates it when you're watching it work!), let the thought go, just like a leaf that's being carried away by a river. This quiet state is when *intuition* can express itself. If you skip this step and launch into your shopping list of what you need today, intuition is not going to happen. How can you listen and talk at the same time?

SECOND: THINK AND ASK: Think about your day ahead and whatever it is that you need to do. Be mindful of others and ask whoever or whatever is your higher power that, as you go through the day, you be directed to do the next right thing, guided by love, tolerance, patience and courage. Try asking only for guidance and acceptance of outcomes rather than drawing up a shopping list of wants. Sometimes you might be over-loaded with stuff going on; remember that you only have this 24 hours and you can get through a day, no matter how tough it seems to be at the time – there is a great saying that I've got plenty of use out of – 'This too shall pass' – everything does, the good, the great, the bad and the terrible. Whatever happens to us, the earth will continue to turn no matter what we think, feel or do. Try this tip: think about something you worried about 12 months ago. Did it actually happen, and if it did, was it as bad as you had feared?

Here's another personal tip. If I have a particularly difficult day in front of me, first I look at the main fact. The day is 24 hours long, and I know I can handle 24 hours of it. Then I reflect on why this day is troubling me. Mentally I work through the inventory process, and ask myself if I'm self-seeking or full of self-centred fear (i.e. that I may lose something or fail to get what I want) or am I being inconsiderate or dishonest? It's always one of those things that is troubling me. Put in language we can instantly understand: *'Will I get the contract, will I lose the contract, will he email me, will she leave, will I get the house, how will she react when I tell her, does he love me, will they find out, I can't believe he did that – how dare he, she's lazy, he's a bastard, I like her, will she do it, I can't afford it – but I want it'*, the list goes on and on. I do try to surrender that thinking and let the defect go – and know that the void will be filled. The solution always comes when I identify the defect. I can then go into my day knowing that I'll at least try to do the right thing because it's for the right reason. This is how I managed to build my company from scratch with no prior knowledge of business, no money and no contacts.

It may be useful to have a few set slogans to help you through a difficult period such as 'Pain means progress', 'Live and let live', 'More will be revealed', 'Expect miracles' or 'Accept the things I cannot change and the wisdom to know the difference.'

Learn them, and when you're in a tight spot repeat them in your head. It works and it takes the heat off momentarily.

Meditation suits some people; personally I find it challenging, but do attempt it. On a personal level my most creative moments come during quiet periods and of course this makes sense – I've made room for great thoughts, because I've cleared the crap from my mind. The crap comes back though, which is why I need to do this every day. If you decide to learn how to meditate, then be aware that you might need to find the right place and conditions for you personally. Initially I sought out local classes, which were a bit of a disaster (a dreary centre on a Tuesday night from 7–8pm just felt a bit weird to me). It worked for others, I hasten to add. I didn't give up though, luckily, and sought out centres when I happened to be in Sri Lanka and Thailand and learned how to meditate there. I wanted to keep the feeling, so I went to great lengths – and while I was doing it, met really interesting people too!

Some people find that keeping a journal is also a good way to help do their morning review. You just write down what you've discovered about any problem you might be facing, and then write the spiritual ways of dealing with it throughout the day. Those who do this find that writing it down reinforces their commitment to living in a different way, and they make quicker progress.

3 MOMENT-BY-MOMENT REVIEW

You can connect to your higher power anywhere you like and whenever you need it throughout the day. Ever had a 'gut feeling' moment? Well, trust it – that's your 'inner resource' trying to tell you something – and it is *always* right. Sit still long enough to notice it. Many of my best business decisions were instinctively made. Sadly, I trusted too many people who swore by spreadsheets and analyses that used to get it incredibly wrong!

• TROUBLESHOOTING: THE 'WHAT • SHOULD I DO?' SYNDROME:

Have you ever been paralysed by indecision? Well today you have a way to deal with it. To get to the right answer you have a choice. You can:

a) try to solve the problem yourself
b) listen to friends and family
c) Google it
d) do nothing
e) try something new.

Let's go for (e), the try something new experiment

First, with your new-found humility, you can accept that it's OK not to know everything. Second, you may even ask someone for help. The most successful people I know have no trouble asking for help, in fact they've honed the skill so well that it's made them a fortune! Third, relax, take it easy, the inspiration will come either from you or someone else, but only if your mind is clear enough to accept the signal.

THE LISTENING EXPERIMENT

You'll need a bit of time in the morning, a pen and paper and the discipline to do this for seven days.

1 Find a quiet place.
2 To listen well, you need to write down everything that comes into your mind, otherwise you might forget things.

Write down thoughts that deal with your family, your work, your community, your domestic duties, your hopes and dreams. You can leave out what you are going to have for breakfast!

3 Look at what you have written.

4 Are these thoughts honest, pure, unselfish, courageous and loving?

5 Take each one that isn't and identify the instinct that has been threatened. Always be mindful to understand your motive behind each one. In other words, are you being selfish, self-centred, dishonest, fearful or inconsiderate?

6 Write down the right thing to do – the answer will come to you if you're not blocking it with your ego.

7 If no guidance comes to you, then there must be something still blocking it. This could be:
  ● a wrong relationship
  ● a wrong that you haven't faced and put right
  ● an indulgence that you just won't give up
  ● anything that you know you should do, but haven't done.
  Put these things right, and try again.

8 The guidance for you will come, not the 'who is right', but the 'what is right'. You'll only see the result of this advice and counsel when you have done what's suggested. This knowledge is no use without action.

If you do this as suggested for seven days you will have accessed the most powerful database of information imaginable – your consciousness and the unlimited power it connects to. The answer to any problem is within you, once you learn how to listen.

• BE RESPONSIBLE FOR THE EFFORT, • NOT THE OUTCOME

We're such control freaks, aren't we? Needing to know the outcome of the things we do. But you know, we really have no idea how things will turn out.

For example, my friends were astonished when I told them that I was about to write a book. Now, I've had some great successes in my life, but not one of them has centred on writing. So they asked how was I going to do it and I told them that I had no idea, I was just going to do it one word at a time. I'm close to the final chapter now. Granted I've had a huge amount of help from my husband Bryan and Rachael, the editor, but I've nearly completed it. Now the question I'm getting asked is 'Will this book be a success?' I don't know; I hope so as it will help a lot of people if it is, but the outcome is really out of my hands. Of course I'll put my fine marketing mind onto it and make a plan, but really I'm powerless over its success.

You see, the road to disappointment is paved with expectation. If I'm living in expectation, I will always be in fear. Why? Because my life and my higher power operate only in the present moment. And when I'm in the present moment, trying to do the next right thing, life is pretty good. It doesn't matter what I have or what I own or what you think of me.

I first got this feeling when I'd been practising these principles for around 12 months. I was 28, unemployed and living in Leeds in a shared student house. Having given up smoking, I'd put on a pile of weight so I used to go the gym most mornings and needed to take the bus to get there. The bus stop was on a busy road that was always clogged with rush hour traffic. I'd make a point of looking at the many faces that sat behind the stationary vehicle steering wheels, and boy, did most of them look miserable. There I was, with nothing materially but a whole lot going on spiritually. Had I touched the fourth dimension? I don't know, all I know is that it was a bloody good feeling.

For the person who tries this step with an open mind, Bill Wilson in his remarkable book, *The Language of the Heart*, describes the other good feelings that will result. He says:

> If he persists, he will almost surely find more serenity, more tolerance, less fear, and less anger. He will acquire a quiet courage, the kind that doesn't strain him. He can look at so-called failure and success for what they really are. Problems and calamity will begin to mean instruction, instead of destruction. He will feel freer and saner. The idea that he may have been hypnotising himself by autosuggestion will become laughable. His sense of purpose and of direction will increase. His tensions and anxieties will begin to fade. His physical health is likely to improve. Wonderful and unaccountable things will start to happen (p. 241).

Come on, who doesn't want some of that?

STEP IN BRIEF

- Staying fulfilled is a continual process of working Steps 1–5.

- A daily spot-check inventory helps you to spot the emotion, identify the instinct, look at your part and hand it over to get relief.

- Self-reflection is a way of living from the inside out, rather than the typical approach of outside in.

Step Seven

PRACTISING THE PRINCIPLES AND PASSING IT ON

• • •

Our deepest fear is not that we are inadequate. Our deepest fear is that we are powerful beyond measure. It is our light, not our darkness, that most frightens us. We ask ourselves, who am I to be brilliant, gorgeous, talented, fabulous? Actually, who are you not to be? ... And as we let our own light shine, we unconsciously give other people permission to do the same. As we're liberated from our own fear, our presence automatically liberates others.

Marianne Williamson, *A Return to Love.*

So here we are. Not quite nirvana, but you're six steps closer.

In this process we're now at the point where we can trust the evidence that this way of life brings results.

So now is the perfect time to rethink your ambitions and align them with your new way of living.

Step 7 is the culmination of this whole programme, meaning you're now at a place where you can be of maximum help to others and yourself.

• • •

PART 1: PRACTISING THE PRINCIPLES

In the past, have you sometimes felt as if you've been wandering through life with no direction? Well, you've just been given a compass. The purpose of this programme so far has been to help you clear out the real or imagined wreckage from your past, and give you a toolkit to move forward with a clear conscience and willing mind. I challenge you now to discover what it is that really makes you happy, and interestingly, you may find that your goal in life will not be based around what you do, but how you feel. Once you feel connected to your purpose (and the proof of the right purpose is that you truly enjoy pursuing it), then new doors will open and marvellous things will begin happening.

This is what happened to me, from that broken wretch of a person in Tokyo to my subsequent fulfilment and success. Nobody could have dared to dream of such a transformation.

This programme works and can rocket you – as it has done me and millions of others – into the fourth dimension. Once I'd begun to understand and submerge my ego and worked to remove my limiting defects on a daily basis, I then had the freedom to dream and create a vision for my life. I made a decision to 'give up' the battle and surrender my life to something more powerful than me. With this evidence that everything in life was going to work out OK, I became fearless (most of the time). I discovered who the real me is, what she enjoys and what her potential is.

I recovered my self-respect and dignity. Once you have this, nobody, other than you, will be able to take it away. It is from here that you can move forward with the power to do, get or be whatever you want. Now you can take this power out from yourself into the world.

• THE LAW OF ATTRACTION: WHAT • YOU BELIEVE, YOU WILL ACHIEVE

This popular theory has morphed out of the findings of quantum physics. In short, we and the world we live in are made of pure vibrating energy. Now, if that's so, then our thoughts are also pure energy and this energy has been scientifically measured. Some thoughts produce high frequency energy, others low frequency. The science of kinesiology takes this further by showing that high frequency thoughts produce a strong physical response, while low frequencies produce a weak response. This means that every thought you have has the potential to strengthen or weaken you. In other words, love, tolerance and forgiveness make you a stronger person, while anger, fear and guilt make you weaker. This is a scientifically proven fact.

If you go back to Step 1 (p. 13), you'll see that I said:

> **This book makes a big promise – perhaps the biggest promise that has ever been made to you: in these pages you'll find a code for living that will help you reach personal fulfilment.**
>
> **The most effective way to achieve this is to begin working a programme that brings you up to the level of 200 or more: the level of courage and integrity.**

This is precisely what we have been aiming at, and that's what the rest of this Step is about: practising love, compassion, courage and integrity – now isn't that attractive?

But there's a saying often heard in 12 Step meetings: 'It works if you work it.' So let's look at how you can work these principles in all areas of your life: at work, with your family, during recreation and social activities and regarding your health.

• WORK & BUSINESS •

We probably spend more hours here than anywhere else, so let's start with our ambitions in work and business.

THE BIG PICTURE

For some of you this may be about changing your job, getting a new career; for others it may be about starting a business or retiring. Whatever it is that you are hoping for though, it's now really down to you – it's your responsibility, and there has never been a better time to figure out what it is that you really want to apply your energies to.

I have found that when you truly know what you want, you can see it, you can feel it; it's as if you have this thing already, it is all that you think about, and it keeps resurfacing in your mind, this then becomes your intention and in a world where like goes to like, we attract what we emit. You'll be at your happiest and most efficient when you know what you should be doing, and you do it to the best of your ability. Your personal success then becomes effortless because it is emanating from true power and not from clawing your way up the ladder of life using brute force. What if you don't know what you should be doing? Good question, and here's the answer: now you know how to ask with the morning exercise in Step 6.

This is exactly what happened to me when I started my own company. Because my life had been changed by travelling and working abroad, I wanted other people to experience what I had. This became my intention. Did I start my company to become a multi-millionaire? No, that wasn't in my mind in the least. I began my company to be of service to others. But it so happened that I had just endured the pain of radical personal growth, and had luckily been shown the principles in this programme. It was exactly (and, I'm convinced, only) because, at almost the same time, I had discovered both this new design for living and realised what I enjoyed doing, that I was able to defy the odds and do it all so well. There is no other explanation for it, given my lack of business experience and relevant skills, other than that I was obviously operating on the right frequency and attracting all the success I could handle.

The road to great things for your career starts here – and you've found a way to make it much easier for you to receive exactly what you want. It's simple. If the findings of Dr David

Hawkins, outlined in Step 1, are true, then 85 per cent of the population on this planet are operating at a level of fear, guilt, shame, anger, pride – in other words a mixed bag of character defects. This means that 15 per cent are the fortunate ones, those that accept responsibility, have courage, show tolerance, compassion and love. Isn't it interesting that this correlates with the division of wealth? You see, charisma is sought after, it carries with it a strong energy field, only a few have it and they attract more of the same, in fact, they generally have abundance in every area of their lives.

Now you know how to join the right party. So the message is simple, keep working this programme and your success – whatever that may be to you – will come automatically because you're supporting your life with high energy patterns.

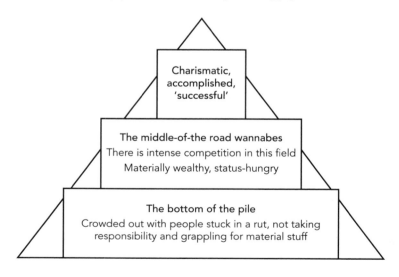

Charismatic, accomplished, 'successful'

The middle-of-the road wannabes
There is intense competition in this field
Materially wealthy, status-hungry

The bottom of the pile
Crowded out with people stuck in a rut, not taking responsibility and grappling for material stuff

THE SMALLER PICTURE

This blue-sky thinking may be OK for some, but you may be thinking that you just want to get on better with your boss, or get more sales, or just get a job. You may have just failed to get that long-awaited promotion, or been made redundant. It's actually in this area of daily living that this programme is the most useful. You can even turn these so called calamities into a learning experience, one that you can eventually share with others. Sometimes those old fears and resentments can keep on haunting you, snatching back your new-found serenity. It is often the little things that people do that can really wind us up, but you now have a method to deal with this, you have a way to handle anything that comes your way. That's what the daily inventory outlined in Step 6 is for.

And what if fortune smiles our way? Keeping level-headed when good news and applause come is just as much a major responsibility as when they don't. Pride and arrogance can slip back as easily as fear and anger if a daily inventory isn't taken. These are low-energy emotions and will attract the same back to you ('Pride goeth before a fall'), so vigilance is the message here. Interestingly, if you look at the most charismatic, accomplished winners of our age, the heads of corporations, Nobel prizewinners, the real movers and shakers of this world, then you'll notice the majority have a 'down to earth-ness', a warmth, an ease. The truly successful consider themselves no better than others because their power comes from 'within'. Remember this when you get the new job, a flashy car, a first-class degree or climb up to the next corporate rung.

At the end of the day, true ambition and success is being content with learning to play well whatever cards have been dealt to you. If you do that, then the rest tends to look after itself.

• YOUR FAMILY •

Families, don't you just love them? Well, don't be surprised if this becomes the most difficult area to turn around. You'd think it would be the easiest, wouldn't you? Sadly no, not in my experience. You see, you have a huge emotional, financial and social investment in your family, and it is because of this that your character defects are more exaggerated. But, of course, it isn't just you that this happens to; it is also true of every member of your family. So what have you got? A bunch of people with character defects on the rampage – either silently or vociferously – all within four walls – now that's what I call Heaven!

This programme can deal with any issue you can throw at it, and that includes your family. The hardest part for you may be the fact that whilst you try to show tolerance, love, patience and responsibility, other members of your family may not respond in kind – their feathers might even be ruffled because you're not 'playing the game' any more. Whatever you do, don't give them this book for their birthday and suggest they start their own personal journey! You had to be ready, and so do they.

Sometimes you may feel as if you're fighting a losing battle. But remember, *this is a selfish programme* – and by that I don't mean that you should be selfish. I mean that you have now taken responsibility for yourself and *you need to protect your new-found serenity and fulfilment*. Tough love is what is sometimes needed in a difficult family situation – that is, the ability to move on, or let go and still love the person.

The same goes for relationships. You may find that, with your new confidence and honesty, you and your partner begin to have different values which cause friction. There are different ways you can choose to deal with this: you can practise acceptance and tolerance, or you can offer moral support for them if they want to try this programme, or you can separate, realising that the two of you are moving toward different paths. I have an old saying: 'Unless a person has had a vital spiritual experience there is little hope of change.' I used it in many situations: with staff, colleagues, my own partner, family members or when I was asked to give advice about other people's relationships. People used to think it was an amusing saying that I pulled out of the bag occasionally, but I knew it was a fact. And so it is with your relationships: nobody changes unless they put the effort in. And you can't put the effort in for them.

This brings me to the interesting anecdote of John. John is in his mid-50s and has been practising these Steps for about a year now. Well known in his family for being highly critical and an out-and-out moaner, he says that he now practises restraint by following his granny's advice: 'If you have nothing positive to say, then don't say anything at all.' So he keeps his mouth shut when he has a critical thought, whereas before he'd just blurt it out. This new way of living for John has culminated in a serious lack of family arguments and silent sulking sessions for some time now. He says he's trying to take this little experiment a bit further and now does his best to even think of something positive to say. John's story is a typical example which shows that this programme takes time and experimentation to get the promised results.

• ROMANTIC RELATIONSHIPS •

Some sage said that there are two kinds of people in the world: people who are not in a relationship and want to get *in*, and people who are in a relationship and want to get *out*! Romantic relationships are so agonising, but we always keep searching. Happily, we can use this programme to make our relationship more fulfilling and longer-lasting.

First, what is love? Is it that swooning feeling we get when we meet the person of our dreams? If that's the case – that love is an emotion – and we know that feelings change, then that's the kind of love that is bound to fade away the moment the rush wears off. And why does that happen? Marianne Williamson, in her fabulous book *A Return to Love*, explains that our first encounter with our partner is where all the ego boundaries drop away and we feel an intense connectedness with the other person. It's like we've known them all along! And we have. . . because we're having a spiritual connection between ourselves and the universe around us.

But is that love? Is this person truly going to satisfy all our emotional needs? Marianne Williamson says, 'A relationship is not meant to be the joining at the hip of two emotional invalids.' Ouch!

So what happens in that romance after the violins stop playing? Well, we take that initial *spiritual* connection and make it *material*. We hand it over to the ego, which grabs it and fills it with fear, and it's like pouring fertiliser on all our character defects. We begin to be critical, intolerant, discovering annoying little character traits that they have.

My husband Bryan tells how he jumped off the relationship merry-go-round by learning to apply this programme to his relationships. Looking for answers, he discussed it with a woman called Jenny who was in a 12 Step programme. Here's what she said – listen up, everybody.

She said the romance that I was seeking was actually pretty selfish. The passionate adventure that I continually sought was based on my own feelings, rather than what I was doing for the other person in the relationship. And if I got gut-wrenchingly honest, my partner was there only to serve my needs. Perhaps, Jenny said, real love is not a feeling but an action: a commitment to behave lovingly toward the other person, do kind things for them, listen to them, and encourage them. I tried this and I began to actually participate in the relationship, to take actions rather than expect things to be done for me: to listen, to encourage, to help, to cheer up, to not give advice, to not criticise, to cuddle. And I discovered that the best foundation for a good relationship is putting the other person's needs first. My selfish mind still occasionally insists, 'But what about *my* needs?' But I've learned to ignore that because I know now that by putting the other person's needs first, invariably my needs get met more than when I make demands.

Try this in a relationship: surrender that romance to a higher purpose and then work through the rest of the Steps in this programme, practising the principles which you already know work: forgiveness, compassion, love and tolerance. You may find that you begin to attract and maintain a more fulfilled relationship. Or that a hot water bottle works nicely.

• PERSONAL HEALTH •

Being the picture of health and feeling great is an inside job. I'm not spouting anything new here. We all know that there is no more effective way to get to optimum health than down and dirty exercise and a well-balanced diet, and there are better people than me to tell you how to do this.

But let's look a little closer, shall we? Let's try to understand how our thoughts and actions do affect our general well-being. Quantum physicists call these 'attractors'. We know that positive attitudes such as tolerance, acceptance, love and compassion are high power attractors – these make your body go strong by releasing brain endorphins. Not so with low power attractors or the 'emergency emotions' of resentment, fear, self-pity, jealousy and so on. These negative attitudes release adrenalin that causes weakness and can even cause damage to certain organs.

So once again, let's look at it from the inside out. Why is our current weight a problem? Because it's injuring our basic instincts of self-esteem and emotional security. Where are we at fault? Perhaps we're being lazy, procrastinating, maybe gluttonous and possibly dishonest with ourselves. What's the solution – hand over these feelings, ask for help, do what's suggested and realise that you can be happy right now, however you look.

Have you ever said to yourself: 'I hope I don't get sick!' and then were frustrated that you promptly got sick? Look at it from the inside. We're saying that out of fear, but if there's one thing I've learned in this process it is that *we are subject to that which we hold in our minds*. Likewise we can attract ill health by being in fear. So change your motives from that of running from illness to running towards health: focus on staying healthy, eat the right foods, get plenty of water and visualise yourself as healthy.

Stress is the scourge of our modern world, but stress is not brought on by external events – it's caused by your reaction to those events. Now you have a simple method to deal with whatever life can throw at you, and here's another promise: if you follow this programme to the best of your ability, your general well-being will improve despite yourself.

Another simple way to avoid feeling stressed is to allow more time. Step 6 can help here. Waking 15 minutes earlier and reflecting on your day is an excellent start. You may even want to set out on your journey to work before the usual time so you can move less hurriedly, this can give you time to collect your thoughts before you go into the office. Take it easy, don't try to overload your day with too much. If you're feeling frayed with the burden of things to do, then do some of them tomorrow, cancel some appointments and don't feel guilty about it! Ask yourself, 'Am I really that indispensable?' or 'How much does it really matter?' If you take it easy like this you'll find that you will have much more energy and focus and, surprisingly, more time.

This is not a licence for unreliability and procrastination though. Taking personal responsibility for your life is still your ultimate goal, but not at the expense of professionalism.

• SOCIAL •

I hope you're not thinking that life is now going to be as dull as dishwater with you mumbling your inventory throughout the day! Not at all. Let me tell you what will probably happen. If you follow this way of life, you'll attract people similar to you. This may mean a parting of the ways for you and some of your old friends, but your life will be filled with other interesting people, social events and hobbies, all of which will be aligned with your new values and interests. Indeed, you'll find that you'll become a better friend, because now you know what true friendship really means – equality rather than power. Petty jealousies, rivalry and trivial arguments need no longer be a barrier to being a good friend. You'll come to see that it's not necessary to be a doormat or the dominant one in a friendship because you've put your life on a true give-and-take basis.

With your new-found self-awareness, why not take action and set about doing what you really like to do, whether that be travelling, sports, writing, dancing or computer games? Join that club or class you've been thinking about for a while but never mustered the courage or found the time for. Or book yourself on that trip you've been dreaming about.

Try to get out and meet people face to face if you can. Conducting your social life via a computer screen may be convenient, but it's no substitute for looking someone in the eye, and no, Skyping someone doesn't count! And today, if you find yourself procrastinating about getting a social life, investigate which defect is being threatened and do something about it. You've got no excuse any more – sorry! Perhaps your ultimate aim in social relationships should now be to figure out what you can bring to the party, rather than what you can take from it.

• OUT AND ABOUT •

I've been fortunate enough to have lived in four countries other than the UK: Japan, China, Australia and Greece. In each one I met other Brits also living there. Without fail, in every country, the general consensus was: 'This is a lovely country, it would be even better without the Japanese (or Chinese, Aussies or Greeks)'! I cringe when I think about this now. It would be just like saying England is a lovely country, it would be even better without the English. In other words, we need to live side by side with people whether we like it or not and, since we're on this journey, we might as well be courteous, kind, patient and tolerant, because this is what's needed as part of the solution instead of the problem.

Let's face it, who likes going to the supermarket? Crowds of people jostling around the chilled food section, bumping into you, you bumping into them. And would you look at that: the woman who went into the 10 items or fewer line with a shopping trolley piled high! Or just when you think you've snuck into the line with the fewest people, the cashier contentedly says 'This till is closed.' You might be one of the lucky few who enjoy this extreme experience of modern life, but for those of us who haven't reached Buddha-hood, let's treat our weekly trip to the local supermarket as a lesson in human behaviour and an area where we can practise these principles. Take it easy when you're shopping, allow a little more time so you don't feel stressed. If a person has a couple of items at the till, let them go before you; smile; be helpful to the little old lady trying to pick up a 5lb bag of potatoes. You'll be amazed how much better you feel.

Now what to do with that pesky parking attendant? First, don't park where you shouldn't – even if you're only nipping into a shop for a cake. Second, if you get a ticket then accept where you're at fault. What is the point in arguing with a person who is doing their job – especially if you have done something wrong? Anyway, have you noticed that your anger generally subsides as soon as you've paid the ticket? So here's a tip – pay up sooner.

How about the faulty goods you want to return? Shouting and swearing at the retailer or service provider may get your refund, but it won't make you feel better. Remember the proven attractor patterns that obey the laws of physics? Anger causes anger, hate destroys the hater and so on. Bear this in mind when you're hopping mad about something that you want to complain about. State your case, firmly and confidently, and use the proper channels as necessary. The result is usually twice as sweet!

What about your nasty neighbour? This area can be as difficult and as sensitive as your family. We recently bought a new house set in large and very overgrown gardens. We don't yet live there as it's being refurbished. In the letterbox I found a letter from my new neighbour. Delighted to have a friendly neighbour, I opened it up and was astonished to see a pretty vicious complaint about how a tree in our overgrown garden had not been cut back and was encroaching on her 'light'. My first reaction was indignant anger – I mean, she didn't even welcome us to the neighbourhood! Instead she just dived into a vitriolic ramble. I told my husband Bryan about this injustice and he calmly said that what was needed was rational action, not hurt feelings. My neighbour was obviously upset, it was our fault, and we owned the offending tree. So I organised for a tree surgeon to come in and cut back the branches. I did the right thing. Now with regard to her not welcoming us to the village, well I'm just judging people by my standards there, aren't I? Not only that, I'm being pretty inconsiderate to want this lady to live as I expect her to – I mean, I've never even met the woman!

The general rule of thumb as you try to live by these principles is to look at the context of any situation and understand your motive. Always ask: am I being selfish, inconsiderate, self-seeking, fearful or dishonest? Then take the right action. But how do I know what is the right action, you may be asking. Deep down, you will *always* know the right thing to do, and if you don't, then flick back to Step 6 to be reminded of what to do in times of indecision.

• ACCEPTANCE: THE ANSWER TO ALL • OUR PROBLEMS

So what do you do when things just aren't going your way and you can't see a solution? When all else fails, the *Big Book of AA* has a great answer:

> And acceptance is the answer to all my problems today. When I am disturbed, it is because I find some person, place, thing or situation – some fact of my life unacceptable to me, and I can find no serenity until I accept that person, place, thing or situation as being exactly the way it is supposed to be at this moment... Unless I accept life completely on life's terms, I cannot be happy. I need to concentrate not so much on what needs to be changed in the world as on what needs to be changed in me and my attitudes (p. 449).

PART 2: PASS IT ON

This programme is both life-affirming and life-changing; it is also full of paradoxes – the ultimate irony being: 'You've got to give it away to keep it.' So far you've taken your problem – whatever you were powerless over – the thing that was keeping you stuck in a rut and unhappy. Then you found the solution and made a decision to take action through the rest of the Steps. What you'll uncover when you get to this Step is that your past problems can be your biggest asset, for the simple reason that you'll have a personal understanding and a lot of experience of how that issue made you live and feel. Interestingly, you'll also discover that you're not alone – that, in fact, you're more like everyone else than you think!

So the next time you come across someone – a friend, a colleague, or a person you meet for a short time on a journey who seems restless, irritable and discontented – you can say 'I've been there and I know how you feel', you can pass on your experience, strength and hope. You see, your new way of life is like a circuit, a flow that needs to keep going out of you. If you keep it to yourself, you'll lose it. This is where you can be of maximum benefit to others and, in giving freely, you'll receive much more in return. I've read that compassion produces one of the highest energy levels. In other words, it makes you (the giver) feel great. On a personal level, working with others is what keeps me coming back to this programme. It just feels good to do good.

• SERVICE AND TIME •

There are many ways that you can be of service to others and it's really important that you find the one with which you feel comfortable and confident. Apart from passing this message on whenever you can, that is – and you'll be surprised how many opportunities are out there. Giving time to a cause or charity is a great way to feel better about yourself, even if you can manage just a few hours. Find something that you're passionate about and there will usually be something that supports it in your local area. These causes will generally be grateful for any assistance you can offer, and the brilliant thing is that you'll be meeting and working with people who are probably on the same path as you. Local schools, hospitals, children's events, elderly centres, fun runs, getting involved in CSR (corporate social responsibility) activities in your company – it all mounts up to getting to that level of fulfilment that you deserve.

Personally I'm involved in a number of charities and causes and I always endeavour to give my time and experience when I'm asked and, yes, I'm probably as busy as you are. You see, I've experienced first-hand that what goes around comes around. What's remarkable about service work is not necessarily what I'm doing; it's the results I get, which always seem to far outweigh the effort. I meet people that I wouldn't ordinarily come across; not only is this fascinating, but it also offers unexpected opportunities for networking and business. Working in a totally different area from the one I'm used to gives me the chance to experience things I'd be highly unlikely to do otherwise.

So today, investigate what's around in your local area – even the act of doing so can be interesting and informative.

• JOIN OR START A LOCAL 7 STEP • GROUP

Many people who follow 12 Step programmes are supported by 'meetings'. Here people with the same issues and objectives come together to study, discuss and share. There are many benefits in attending this kind of meeting. First, there is more wisdom in the collective consciousness of a group than an individual; in other words, a problem shared is a problem solved. Second, joining a group provides camaraderie and friendship; and third, it's great fun – honest!

The format is simple and practical and is modelled on the setup of thousands of 12 Step groups across the world. More details on how to find a group in your area or to set one up can be found on www.thepersonalrevolution.net. You also have the opportunity to find or become a virtual guide on this site.

• PRINCIPLES FOR LIVING •

So here we are, at the end of the Steps and the beginning of a new way of life. Both you and I have been given a set of principles by which to live. These are not new, they've been with humanity since time began; I suppose you could call them the 'directions' that tell us how to be fully human in an ever-changing world. They are the key to right values and attitudes and in turn these are the key to right actions that open the door to right living. It follows, then, that if we can live by these principles in all our affairs, we'll be peaceful, content and fulfilled.

It works if you work it.

This is a promise from the millions of people whose lives have changed because they've *worked* this programme of actions.

STEP IN BRIEF

- Practise these principles in all of your affairs – with progress, not perfection, being your goal.
- Give it away to keep it.
- Right attitudes lead to right actions; right actions lead to right living; and right living leads to fulfilment.

I'll leave you with a simple but brilliant manifesto for daily living:

• JUST FOR TODAY •

Just for today I will try to live through this day only, and not tackle my whole life problem at once. I can do something for 12 hours that would appal me if I felt that I had to keep it up for a lifetime.

Just for today I will be happy. Most people are as happy as they make up their mind to be.

Just for today I will adjust myself to what is, and not try to adjust everything to my own desires. I will take my 'luck' as it comes and fit myself into it.

Just for today I will try to strengthen my mind. I will study. I will learn something useful. I will not be a mental loafer. I will read something that requires effort, thought and concentration.

Just for today I will exercise my soul in three ways: I will do somebody a good turn, and not get found out; if anybody knows of it, it will not count. I will do at least two things that I don't want to – just for the sake of it. I will not show anyone that my feelings are hurt; they may be hurt, but today I will not show it.

Just for today I will be agreeable. I will look as well as I can, dress becomingly, talk quietly, act courteously, criticise not one bit, not find fault with anything and not try to improve or regulate anybody except myself.

Just for today I will have a programme. I may not follow it exactly, but I will have it. I will save myself from two pests: hurry and indecision.

Just for today I will have a quiet half-hour all by myself, and relax. During this half-hour, I will try to get a better perspective on my life.

Just for today I will be unafraid. Especially I will not be afraid to enjoy what is beautiful, and to believe that as I give to the world, so the world will give to me.

APPENDIX 1: WHAT IS AA?

• • •

AA, the original 12 Step recovery movement, came into being in the mid 1930s through a synchronicity of events.

• EVENT 1: THE PROBLEM REVEALED •

In 1934 a New York stockbroker and chronic alcoholic called Bill Wilson was at the end of his rope. Although an intelligent, talented and driven individual, he was facing the certainty that he would have to be locked up or die from his drinking.

In one of his last binges he was open-minded enough to ask America's leading specialist in alcoholism, Dr William Silkworth, what his problem was. Silkworth compared his inability to control drinking as an allergy (defined in the dictionary as 'an abnormal reaction') in that after he succumbed to the desire to drink, a 'phenomenon of craving develops. . . unless this person can experience an entire psychic change there is very little hope of his recovery'. *Alcoholics Anonymous* (p. xxvii).

With this information, Bill was fully aware of the problem, but needed to find a solution to avoid having a drink in the first place. His drinking continued.

• EVENT 2: THE SOLUTION REVEALED •

Meanwhile a successful investment banker named Rowland Hazzard was experiencing the same turmoil. Although unaware of the nature of the problem, in desperation he sought out the founder of analytical psychology, Carl Jung.

Jung stressed that he had never seen one single alcoholic case recover, but there were exceptions, and the only solution lay in a 'vital spiritual experience', what he called,

> **huge emotional displacements and rearrangements.**
> **Ideas, emotions, and attitudes which were once the**
> **guiding forces of the lives of these men are suddenly**
> **cast to one side and a completely new set of**
> **conceptions and motives begin to dominate them.**

Typically these people had given themselves to a spiritual organisation and surrendered to a power greater than themselves, which relieved their alcoholic obsession.

With this chink of hope Hazzard went back to the US and sought out the spiritual solution that Jung had discussed. He found a society called The Oxford Groups, a spiritual movement for people who felt disillusioned with materialism that gained ground during the Depression. They met regularly to discuss living by spiritual principles of humility, honesty and service. Rowland Hazzard recovered through these groups.

• EVENT 3: THE PROGRAMME OF • ACTION CREATED

Hazzard then passed the message he'd learned from Jung to his friend Ebby Thatcher, who was also a hopeless alcoholic. Ebby became sober. This example of one person helping another was then passed via Ebby to his boyhood friend Bill Wilson, who by this time understood the problem, but not the solution. Ebby told Bill that recovery depended on honesty, humility, service to others and accepting a power greater than himself.

A firm atheist, Bill found the whole notion objectionable, fell into a deep depression, and continued to drink alcoholically until he was hospitalised again, this time with a prognosis of sure death. While in hospital Bill admitted defeat, he gave in and, when he did this, a 'profound peace' came over him and the desire to drink was lifted.

Bill was quick to see how his experience could benefit others and went to work passing on the message he'd learned from Ebby. Realising that alcoholics needed a clear plan of action, he devised 12 Steps as an amplification of the Steps from The Oxford Groups. Small groups of individuals began meeting together to support each other and AA quickly spread around the world.

• TODAY •

- AA is established in 180 countries around the world.
- Its 12 Steps are the single most effective programme of recovery for those with alcohol addiction.
- The number of other recovery programmes that have sprung from AA is more than 250.
- Bill Wilson is credited with being one of the 100 greatest Americans who ever lived and is recognised as being the founder of the entire global 'recovery' movement.

• THE 12 STEPS •

You'll notice that God is the specified higher power in these original steps. Although this may sound religious, a very significant number of atheists and agnostics can be counted among the millions who have followed this programme.

These are the original 12 Steps as published by Alcoholics Anonymous.

1 We admitted we were powerless over alcohol – that our lives had become unmanageable.
2 Came to believe that a power greater than ourselves could restore us to sanity.
3 Made a decision to turn our will and our lives over to the care of God as we understood Him.
4 Made a searching and fearless moral inventory of ourselves.
5 Admitted to God, to ourselves, and to another human being the exact nature of our wrongs.
6 Were entirely ready to have God remove all these defects of character.
7 Humbly asked Him to remove our shortcomings.
8 Made a list of all persons we had harmed, and became willing to make amends to them all.
9 Made direct amends to such people wherever possible, except when to do so would injure them or others.
10 Continued to take personal inventory and when we were wrong promptly admitted it.
11 Sought through prayer and meditation to improve our conscious contact with God as we understood Him, praying only for knowledge of His Will for us and the power to carry that out.

12 Having had a spiritual awakening as the result of these Steps, we tried to carry this message to alcoholics, and to practise these principles in all our affairs.

ACKNOWLEDGEMENT

The 12 Steps and brief excerpts from *Alcoholics Anonymous* the *Twelve Steps and the Twelve Traditions* and *The Language of the Heart* are reprinted with permission of Alcoholics Anonymous World Services, Inc. (AAWS). Permission to reprint brief excerpts from the material stated above does not mean that AAWS has reviewed or approved the contents of this publication, or that AAWS necessarily agrees with the views expressed herein. AA is a programme of recovery from alcoholism *only* – use of the 12 Steps in connection with programmes and activities that are patterned after AA, but which address other problems, or in any other non–AA context, does not imply otherwise.

APPENDIX 2:
INVENTORY SHEETS

...

Review of Resentments

INSTRUCTIONS FOR COMPLETION

Action 1: List all of the names of people, institutions or values that you believe have wronged you. (NB Complete column 1 from top to bottom. Do nothing on columns 2, 3 or 4 until column 1 is complete.)

Action 2: List all of the harms on your grudge list that these people, places and things have done. Write this down one at a time. (NB Complete column 2 from top to bottom. Do nothing on columns 3 or 4 until column 2 is complete.)

Action 3: On your grudge list put a tick in each square that names your injuries. Was it your self-esteem, your security, your ambitions, your personal and sexual relations that had been interfered with? (NB Complete each column within column 3 going from top to bottom, starting with the self-esteem column and finishing with the sexual ambitions column. Do nothing on column 4 until column 3 is complete.)

Action 4: Putting out of your mind the wrongs others had done, look for your own mistakes. Where had you been selfish, dishonest, self-seeking, and frightened and inconsiderate? (**Asking yourself the above questions, complete each column within column 4.**)

Action 5: Reading from left to right, now see the resentment (column 1), the cause (column 2), the part of self that had been affected (column 3), and the exact nature of the defect within you that allowed the resentment to surface and block you (column 4).

COLUMN 1	COLUMN 2
I'm resentful at:	The cause:
1	
2	
3	

SELF'

COLUMN 3				COLUMN 4			
Affects my… (Which part of self caused the resentment?)				What is the exact nature of my wrongs, faults, mistakes, defects, shortcomings?			
Social Instinct	Security Instinct	Sex Instinct	Ambitions				
Personal relationships	Material / Emotional	Acceptable sex relations / Hidden sex relations	Social / Security / Sexual	Selfish	Dishonest	Self-seeking/ Frightened	Inconsiderate

Review of Fears

INSTRUCTIONS FOR COMPLETION

Action 1: List all of the names of people, institutions or values that you believe have wronged you. (**NB Complete column 1 from top to bottom. Do nothing on columns 2, 3 or 4 until column 1 is complete.**)

Action 2: List all of the harms on your grudge list that these people, places and things have done. Write this down one at a time. (**NB Complete column 2 from top to bottom. Do nothing on columns 3 or 4 until column 2 is complete.**)

Action 3: On your grudge list put a tick in each square that names your injuries. Was it your self-esteem, your security, your ambitions, your personal and sexual relations that had been interfered with? (**NB Complete each column within column 3 going from top to bottom, starting with the self-esteem column and finishing with the sexual ambitions column. Do nothing on column 4 until column 3 is complete.**)

Action 4: Putting out of your mind the wrongs others had done, look for your own mistakes. Where had you been selfish, dishonest, self-seeking, and frightened and inconsiderate? (**Asking yourself the above questions, complete each column within column 4.**)

Action 5: Reading from left to right, now see the resentment (column 1), the cause (column 2), the part of self that had been affected (column 3), and the exact nature of the defect within you that allowed the resentment to surface and block you (column 4).

COLUMN 1	COLUMN 2
I'm resentful at:	The cause:
1	
2	
3	

SELF'									COLUMN 4			
COLUMN 3												
Affects my… (Which part of self caused the resentment?)									What is the exact nature of my wrongs, faults, mistakes, defects, shortcomings?			
Social Instinct	Security Instinct	Sex Instinct			Ambitions							
Personal relationships	Material	Emotional	Acceptable sex relations	Hidden sex relations	Social	Security	Sexual		Selfish	Dishonest	Self-seeking/ Frightened	Inconsiderate

Review of Sexual Conduct

INSTRUCTIONS FOR COMPLETION

Action 1: List all of the names of people, institutions or values that you believe have wronged you. (NB Complete column 1 from top to bottom. Do nothing on columns 2, 3 or 4 until column 1 is complete.)

Action 2: List all of the harms on your grudge list that these people, places and things have done. Write this down one at a time. (NB Complete column 2 from top to bottom. Do nothing on columns 3 or 4 until column 2 is complete.)

Action 3: On your grudge list put a tick in each square that names your injuries. Was it your self-esteem, your security, your ambitions, your personal and sexual relations that had been interfered with? (NB Complete each column within column 3 going from top to bottom, starting with the self-esteem column and finishing with the sexual ambitions column. Do nothing on column 4 until column 3 is complete.)

Action 4: Putting out of your mind the wrongs others had done, look for your own mistakes. Where had you been selfish, dishonest, self-seeking, and frightened and inconsiderate? (**Asking yourself the above questions, complete each column within column 4.**)

Action 5: Reading from left to right, now see the resentment (column 1), the cause (column 2), the part of self that had been affected (column 3), and the exact nature of the defect within you that allowed the resentment to surface and block you (column 4).

COLUMN 1	COLUMN 2
I'm resentful at:	The cause:
1	
2	
3	

SELF' COLUMN 3									COLUMN 4			
ffects my… Which part of self caused the esentment?)									What is the exact nature of my wrongs, faults, mistakes, defects, shortcomings?			
ocial nstinct	Security Instinct	Sex Instinct			Ambitions							
Personal relationships	Material	Emotional	Acceptable sex relations	Hidden sex relations	Social	Security	Sexual		Selfish	Dishonest	Self-seeking/ Frightened	Inconsiderate

Review of Harms

INSTRUCTIONS FOR COMPLETION

Action 1: List all of the names of people, institutions or values that you believe have wronged you. (NB Complete column 1 from top to bottom. Do nothing on columns 2, 3 or 4 until column 1 is complete.)

Action 2: List all of the harms on your grudge list that these people, places and things have done. Write this down one at a time. (NB Complete column 2 from top to bottom. Do nothing on columns 3 or 4 until column 2 is complete.)

Action 3: On your grudge list put a tick in each square that names your injuries. Was it your self-esteem, your security, your ambitions, your personal and sexual relations that had been interfered with? (NB Complete each column within column 3 going from top to bottom, starting with the self-esteem column and finishing with the sexual ambitions column. Do nothing on column 4 until column 3 is complete.)

Action 4: Putting out of your mind the wrongs others had done, look for your own mistakes. Where had you been selfish, dishonest, self-seeking, and frightened and inconsiderate? (**Asking yourself the above questions, complete each column within column 4.**)

Action 5: Reading from left to right, now see the resentment (column 1), the cause (column 2), the part of self that had been affected (column 3), and the exact nature of the defect within you that allowed the resentment to surface and block you (column 4).

COLUMN 1	COLUMN 2
I'm resentful at:	The cause:
1	
2	
3	

SELF'									
COLUMN 3							COLUMN 4		
ffects my… Which part of self caused the esentment?)							What is the exact nature of my wrongs, faults, mistakes, defects, shortcomings?		
ocial astinct	Security Instinct	Sex Instinct			Ambitions				
Personal relationships	Material	Emotional	Acceptable sex relations	Hidden sex relations	Social	Security	Sexual	Selfish	Dishonest	Self-seeking/ Frightened	Inconsiderate

APPENDIX 3: FULFILLED – NOTES FOR GUIDES

...

What an exciting thought: we can pass on to others what we have learned and, by doing so, we can play a small part in this continuum of growth.

There are many reasons for doing this:

1 By sharing your experience with a newcomer, your appreciation of the programme and its impact on your life deepens.
2 By listening to others' experiences, you are reminded of where you were when you started, encouraging you to grow a little more.
3 It helps to keep you on the path; when you 'talk the talk', you become more fully aware that you need to 'walk the walk' as well.
4 By giving of yourself to others, you'll feel the satisfaction of having a bond with new people who really need your help.
5 By helping others, you give away what you have received.

Being a guide may sound intimidating, but as Dr Patrick Carnes expresses it brilliantly in *A Gentle Path through the Twelve Steps*, 'there are only a few things you need to do:

1 Work hard to understand the whole story of the person you are sponsoring.

2 Give emotional support to the person you are sponsoring during those difficult times.

3 Help the person you are sponsoring to focus on the basics of your particular program.

4 Help the person you are sponsoring to focus on the Steps of the program.'

As a guide your main task is just to be there for them as they take those first baby steps. It is a serious commitment, but this doesn't mean that you need to dash over to their house at 2am to hold their hand. Most guides set aside a block of time, say two hours a week, to get together and go through the Steps. Remember also that you can volunteer to be a virtual guide. In this case you would:

- share your experience of finding a higher power (whatever that is)
- help them discover their basic instincts
- listen to their inventories
- help them to spot their character defects
- assist with making their amends list, and become willing to set things right, and most importantly
- give them an encouraging word or two to stay the course.

Before starting to guide them, it would help for you to take another look at how you see and experience the programme (it is, after all, a personal journey). As you help this person, you will be finding good things about them that they overlook. Make a conscious effort to help them see what it is that they are doing right. Often we see only the bad in ourselves, so you can give them a priceless gift.

• SO WHERE DO I START? •

- Work through the 7 Steps yourself.
- Offer to be a guide to anyone you know that may be interested in this programme of action.
- Visit www.thepersonalrevolution.net and sign up as an anonymous personal guide to others.

NOTE FOR GUIDES WHO HAVEN'T WORKED THIS PROGRAMME

Become familiar with this book, especially Steps 2–5, and read this Appendix again.

REFERENCES

...

Anonymous. *Alcoholics Anonymous*. Alcoholics Anonymous Publishing Inc., New York, 1955).

Aurelius, Marcus. *Meditations: Living, Dying and the Good Life.* Orion Publishing Group, London (2003).

Carnes, Patrick. *A Gentle Path through the Twelve Steps.* Hazelden, HQ, Center City (MN) (1993).

Dyer, Wayne. *The Power of Intention.* Hay House, Inc., Carlsbad, CA, USA (2004).

Hawkins, David. *Power vs Force: The hidden determinants of human behaviour.* Hay House, Inc., Carlsbad, CA (1995).

Keane, Fergal. *All of These People.* HarperCollins, London (2005).

McQ, Joe (McQuany). *Carry This Message*, August House, Inc., NE (2002).

McQ, Joe. *The Steps We Took.* August House, Inc., NE (1990).

van Hooft, Stan. *Life, Death and Subjectivity*, Rodopi, Amsterdam (2004).

Williamson, Marianne. *A Return to Love.* HarperCollins, New York (1994).

Wilson, Bill. *The Language of the Heart.* Alcoholics Anonymous Publishing, Inc., New York (1988).

Wilson, Bill. *The Twelve Steps and the Twelve Traditions.* Alcoholics Anonymous Publishing, Inc., New York (1952).

REALLY USEFUL INFORMATION

•••

www.thepersonalrevolution.net – **The Global Community of Life-Changers**

The meeting place of like-minded people and a natural progression from this book. It's really simple to use and you can create your own profile, post and comment on blogs, chat, find or start a local 7 Step Group and a virtual guide. You can also complete and keep your Inventory Sheets and store them safely in your own personal vault.

www.deirdrebounds.com – **Internationally Acclaimed Speaker**

Deirdre Bounds is an exceptional Speaker and specialises in the areas of Motivation, Enterprise & Entrepreurship, Women in Business and Raising Aspirations of Young People. She also gives an entertaining keynotes speech on the 7 Steps as well as half day, full day and weekend workshops on the subject.

www.partiesaroundtheworld.co.uk – **Ethical Gift Giving for Children's Parties**

This is Deirdre's new passion and business. Disillusioned by the material nature of children's parties, Deirdre has set up a Web-based solution to help both the parents of the party thrower and the party goer. Little things like automated invitations, RSVPs and thank-you notes save time, but most importantly themed parties with donation-based gift giving around great causes that children will understand, such as wildlife and education. If you've got children, check it out.